NORTHRUP

The Life of

Sir William Northrup McMillan

1872-1925

By Judy Aldrick

Published by Old Africa Books
A division of Kifaru Educational and Editorial Consultants LTD
PO Box 65, Kijabe, 00220, Kenya

Printed in Nairobi by The Regal Press Kenya Ltd.

A NOTE ON THE PRINCIPAL SOURCES USED AND ACKNOWLEDGEMENTS

Researching for this book has been a challenging, but an ultimately satisfying process. This is the first biography that has been written about William Northrup McMillan, so there were no previous accounts I could look to for inspiration. He left no personal papers and had no surviving siblings or children so there were no close family members whom I could consult. Consequently, I have had to start from the beginning and my researches have led me to many surprising sources over the two years I have followed his trail. Although his name appears in almost every account of early colonial Kenya, and he is mentioned in most of the narratives of big game hunting, the details are sparse and the man is shadowy, buried beneath layers of myth and hearsay. To reach through to the man himself and disentangle fact from fiction has been like making a jigsaw puzzle, where pieces are lost and there is no picture to work from. It has been a fascinating journey of discovery. I have had to stalk my prey in three different continents, in Africa, Europe and the USA. At times he disappeared altogether, hidden from view, only to turn up unexpectedly. Over the years he has been forgotten and memories have become distorted, but now it is high time his story be told and the true facts of his life be revealed.

SOURCES

My most fruitful source has been the McMillan scrapbooks, which are held on microfilm in Rhodes House Library. These consist of two scrapbooks, which belonged to Lucie McMillan, the wife of Northrup

McMillan. They contain a random selection of newspaper cuttings and letters recording events in their lives and those of their friends, much of which Lucie put together after the death of her husband. They are not always in chronological order and the date and name of the source is sometimes missing, but in the absence of any other contemporary documentary evidence, they are the next best thing. I tried hard to locate the originals, which were at one time in the possession of Lucie McMillan's great nephew's second wife, Mrs Margaret Maxwell, but the trail went cold, as there were no children from the marriage.

My most exciting find was a diary of a safari and a visit to Northrup McMillan in 1921, which is amongst the Bixby papers held in the Washington University in St Louis, Special Collections. This I made the subject of an entire chapter as it provided a rare first hand account of the McMillan's day-to-day life in Kenya.

His childhood and early life presented me with the greatest problems, as I could find virtually no information at all, not even a registration of birth. There were few written records in Missouri of the mid to late 19th century and Northrup, the sickly child of immigrant parents, passed under the radar. I went to St Louis to investigate and see what could be found. I saw the family home and visited the local history museum and public libraries seeking enlightenment. More information came to light. I learnt about his early schooling and how a brother and sister died in infancy and gained a clearer impression of what St Louis was like in the late Victorian era. The on-line referenced records of the local newspaper *The St Louis Post-Dispatch* were most helpful. I managed to trace his secondary school, but no relevant documents were available. His time in New Mexico recovering from suspected TB remained vague in the extreme. Even his early manhood in St Louis working in his father's factory was unrecorded as the company paperwork was lost.

Once he arrived in Europe documentation became more forthcoming, and my spirits lifted further when I found the two books commissioned by Northrup recording his expeditions to Sudan and Ethiopia. These were a complete revelation as I had no idea Northrup McMillan had been an explorer before arriving in Kenya. These provided exciting material for two of the next chapters.

President Roosevelt's famous safari in 1909 also provided me with good information about Northrup and his farm and hunting lodge at Juja. Descriptions and accounts of Juja turned up in several contemporary safari and hunting narratives. I was also pleased to find letters to Northrup amongst the Roosevelt papers held in the Library of Congress. One letter in particular was of interest as this was from Northrup (a rare occurrence) describing his activities during World War I.

Northrup's military service during World War I, for which he received a knighthood, was also reasonably well documented, but the last few years of his life presented more challenges. For this I had to delve into colonial politics to understand the issues at stake and assess his involvement and input. Elspeth Huxley's books about Kenya and her biography of Lord Delamere were an invaluable source as it gave me insight into the politics and thinking of the early settlers.

On my various trips to Kenya I visited the houses where Northrup lived, the places he frequented and the mountaintop where he was buried. Here the imprint of the man could still be felt and the impulses of the enormous and generous American is understood.

Running throughout the book is a historical narrative, describing the geo-political map of Africa and the early colonial period in Kenya, I make no apologies for this as it provides essential background, and perspective for the life of Northrup McMillan. Touched upon lightly is also the fashionable Edwardian lifestyle led by the wealthy of the period and enjoyed by an American millionaire, who in the end preferred to live in Africa.

ACKNOWLEDGEMENTS

D uring the course of my researches I have had to consult many people, libraries and institutions.

To the staff of Rhodes House Library, Oxford; Washington University in St Louis Special Collections and Libraries; The Compton Public Library, St Louis; The Missouri Historical Society Research Library; The University of Missouri Library; The McMillan Library, Nairobi; The Royal Geographical Society, London; Quex House Library, Birchington, Kent; the Library of Congress, Washington DC; The Hill School, Pottstown; The Martin and Osa Johnson Safari Museum, Kansas; The Central Chancery of the order of Knighthood, St James's Place, London; Westminster Library; The East African Women's League; and the Bellefontaine Cemetery I extend my sincerest thanks.

My especial gratitude goes to all those who have shared information and memories, lent photographs and suggested leads. Your input has brought life to the book and fleshed out the chief character and without your help, this could not have been achieved. In particular I would like to mention Christine Nicholls, Elwood Taylor, Dorothy Balean, Johnnie Nettlefold, the late Cynthia Salvadori, Errol Trzebinski, Jane Carver, Mike Destro, Pilly Turner, Douglas Duncan, Andrew Buchanan, Dr Pascal Imperato, Robin Cockett, Steve Mills, Jane Rose, Max Morgan-Witts, Robert Soper, John Sutton, Shariffa Keshavjee, Hazel Basford, Anne Phythian-Adams, Rachel Wells, Dick & Julia Moss, Sonya Rooney, Sarah Schnuriger, Dick Daniels, Gary Farrant, Edward Paice, Jacquelyn Borgeson, Cynthia Millar and Adele Heagney.

The internet has proved an invaluable source, allowing me to read rare books and search records on line thus enabling me to do my research far quicker and more conveniently than in the past. The ease in which digital photographs can now be sent and reproduced has helped enormously in finding illustrative material. The ancestry website has been of particular help and I have been able to access libraries in Canada, USA and Britain, while sitting comfortably at home in Kent.

I would like to make special mention of my husband, Clive, for his patience and forbearance and for all the many cups of tea he made for me while I worked at my computer. Last but not least I thank Shel Arensen of Old Africa books, who first suggested that I write about Northrup McMillan, a subject which would not have occurred to me, and then gave me quiet encouragement and never failing support whenever I wavered in my quest.

Judy Aldrick
Kent, UK

CONTENTS

LIST OF ILLUSTRATIONS

I have made strenuous attempts to contact all copyright holders of the following photographs and if there are any I have inadvertently missed or wrongly attributed I sincerely apologise and will rectify this in any subsequent editions.

Page 58: Advance publicity for McMillan's Expedition to Ethiopia. *St Louis Post-Dispatch Newspaper Archive*

Page 60: Sir John Harrington with Ras Mkonnen on his visit to England in 1902. *Victoria and Albert Museum, London*

Page 61: Map of Sudan and Ethiopia showing the Nile River and the area where Northrup travelled on his explorations.

Page 66: Major Powell Cotton in hunting attire. *Powell Cotton Museum*

Page 67: Steel boat in sections.

Page 68: Map of Ethiopia showing the rivers and areas explored by Northrup during the years 1902-5.

Page 70: Baluchi ivory traders c1900. *Powell Cotton Museum*

Page 74: John Destro and the Willsden Tent. *Mike Destro*

Page 78: The Fort at Fashoda. *Powell Cotton Museum*

Page 80: The Sobat towing the smaller boats up the Nile. *from B H Jessen 'McMillan's Expeditions'.*

Page 82: Lucie McMillan posing as Diana the huntress on the banks of the Nile. *Mike Destro*

Page 84: Louise Decker riding her mule in Ethiopia. *Mike Destro*

Page 92: Northrup McMillan at Mombasa Railway Station. *Mike Destro*

Page 93: View of Mombasa c.1904, showing the Mombasa Club in the foreground. *From a private collection*

Page 95: Cartoon of the 'Lunatic Line' the railway in the early days. *from Lord Cranworth 'Profit and Sport in East Africa'*

Page 97: Charles Bulpett (left) with Northrup on their first hunting trip to Kenya in 1904. *From B H Jessen 'McMillan's Expeditions'*

Page 98: The original farm house at Long Juju. *Johnnie Nettlefold*

Page 99: A photographic portrait of Northrup McMillan in 1904. *from 'The Reveille'*

Page 100: View of Ol Donyo Sabuk with campsite. *Powell Cotton Museum*

Page 103: Moving Equipment to the farm at Juja. *Mike Destro*

Page 113: A newspaper depiction of McMillan's Juja Estate. *St Louis Post-Dispatch*

Page 114: An early view of Juja Farmhouse, showing the kitchen extension at the back and the ladders to the attic where safari equipment was stored. *Mike Destro*

Page 115: The bachelor's quarters at Juja. *Johnny Nettlefold*

Page 116: Front Cover of the Sales Brochure for McMillan's Estate at Juja. *Johnnie Nettlefold*

Page 117: A later view of Juja Farmhouse showing the gardens leading down to the Ruera River. *Johnnie Nettlefold*

Page 117: A View of Juja House taken in 2011. *Judy Aldrick*

Page 117: End View of Juja House taken in 2011. *Judy Aldrick*

Page 118: Juja Estate map from the Sales Brochure. *Johnnie Nettlefold*

Page 119: Louise Decker on the steps at Juja. Note the iron piles and panel construction. *Mike Destro*

Page 119: Lucie McMillan on horseback with Juja house in the background. *Mike Destro*

Page 121: St Louis Newspapers ran articles about Roosevelt's upcoming safari. *St Louis Post-Dispatch*

Page 123: Northrup and Lucie McMillan sitting on the steps of Juja House with Teddy Roosevelt. *Johnnie Nettlefold*

Page 125: Lucie McMillan with her pet cheetah at Juja. *Johnnie Nettlefold*

Page 126: The stables at Juja with horses and their syces. *Johnnie Nettlefold*

Page 128: Northrup kept a pet lion at Juja. *Dorothy Balean*

Page 130: Northrup McMillan (right) with the hunter RJ Cunninghame checking safari supplies for Prince Wilhelm of Sweden. *Nigel Pavitt*

Page 131: Winston Churchill stuck in the mud at Athi in 1907. *from 'My African Journey'*

Page 131: Northrup with his pet warthog. *Johnnie Nettlefold*

Page 136: Chiromo House in the McMillan era. *Bixby Diary, Washington University in St Louis*

Page 137: Lucie McMillan playing with her dogs in the garden at Chiromo. *Bixby Diary, Washington University in St Louis*

Page 139: Chiromo House in the University of Nairobi Campus in 2011. *photo by Judy Aldrick*

Page 142: The wedding of Violet Donkin to Donald Sharpe at Chiromo in 1917. *Errol Trzebinski*

Page 144: McMillan in his buckboard drawn by white Abyssinian mules in front of Juja House. *Johnnie Nettlefold*

Page 148: The Convention of Associations, which met in Nairobi in 1913. *Stephen Mills*

Page 157: The McMillan's Mayfair House at 19, Hill Street, London, in 2011. *Judy Aldrick*

Page 162: The McMillan Mausoleum at Bellefontaine Cemetery, St Louis. *Judy Aldrick*

Page 172: Frederick Courteney Selous, DSO. *from Millais biography of Selous*

Page 173: Northrup McMillan in military uniform, 1915. *Stephen Mills*

Page 174: Northrup McMillan with his friend Ewart Grogan. *Old Africa*

Page 176: Military top brass visit Chiromo when it was a convalescent home during World War I. *Stephen Mills*

Page 180: African labourers waiting for their wages at Juja Farm. *Mike Destro*

Page 180: Kikuyu women dancing for joy round the bag of maize they have been given for working at Juja Farm c.1907. *Mike Destro*

Page 185: A M Jeevanjee on the steps of his house in Nairobi with General Smuts. *Zarina Patel*

Page 187: Lord Delamere. *Elspeth Huxley 'White Man's Country'*

Page 196: McMillan's Donyo Sabuk House under construction in 1921. *Bixby Diary, Washington University in St Louis.*

Page 201: Northrup McMillan near Narok. *Bixby Diary, Washington University in St Louis*

Page 203: The rear of Donyo Sabuk House undergoing repairs in 2010. *Judy Aldrick*

Page 204: African labourers dig the garden at McMillan's Donyo Sabuk house. *Bixby Diary, Washington University in St Louis*

Page 209: McMillan's traction engine used for ploughing and bringing sisal to the factory at Donyo Sabuk. *Douglas Duncan*

Page 210: Sisal plants at Donyo Sabuk farm with the manager E L Lindsay (right) and his wife (centre). *Douglas Duncan*

Page 212: Lady Lucie McMillan in 1921. *H K (pop) Binks.*

Page 214: Northrup McMillan in his later years. *From 'The Reveille'*

Page: 219: Osa and Martin Johnson on Safari. *From 'Four Years in Paradise'*

Page 224: Northrup McMillan's grave on the mountain, Ol Donyo Sabuk. *Judy Aldrick*

Page 225: One of the McMillan cars on Ol Donyo Sabuk. The radiator has boiled and has stopped for a refill on the climb up the mountain. *Pilly Turner*

Page 226: View of the original mugumo tree beside the grave. The tree is no longer there. *Pilly Turner*

Page 226: Close up view of McMillan's tombstone showing where the grave was vandalised and the plaque removed. *Judy Aldrick*

Page 230: Laying the Foundation Stone for the McMillan Memorial Library in 1929. *Stephen Mills*

Page 230: The Official opening of the McMillan Memorial Library in 1931. *Stephen Mills*

Page 231: The McMillan Memorial Library in 2011 in busy downtown Nairobi. *Judy Aldrick*

Page 231: The stone lions that flank the library steps were donated by Sir John and Lady Harrington. *Judy Aldrick*

Page 232: Duke of Aosta and Lady McMillan on Ol Donyo Sabuk. *Pilly Turner*

Page 234: Lady Lucie McMillan is presented to Princess Elizabeth in Nairobi in 1952. *Pilly Turner*

INTRODUCTION

He strode down the platform with a purposeful step, a giant of a man, weighing 20 stone and standing six foot three inches tall. He towered over the white clad officials waiting to see the train depart, who hastily stood aside to let him pass. The heat and rush caused beads of perspiration to break out on his forehead, which he brushed away with an impatient hand. He pushed his solar topee further back on his head, revealing a flushed, sunburnt face, with dark moustache and brown eyes, fixed and intent.

"Hurry Hurry!" he admonished the porter, who was struggling with a mountain of luggage piled upon a makeshift wooden cart. "The train is about to leave."

The drawled, transatlantic vowels betrayed the origin of the man, while the array of guns and ammunition he carried with him disclosed the reason for his journey so far from home. He was an American, a big game hunter on a shooting expedition. The man was William Northrup McMillan aged 32, the year 1904, the month September, and the place Mombasa, British East Africa.

A photograph survives in the Destro Collection, showing Northrup at this time walking along the platform in Mombasa. With hat pushed back, shirtsleeves casually unbuttoned, and large stomach pushed forward, the imposing presence of the man is clear to see.

Northrup had travelled far from his hometown of St Louis, Missouri. As an American citizen he was a somewhat unusual visitor to British East Africa, which at this embryonic stage had not even attained colonial status, being still merely a protectorate. But Northrup was a man, with advanced ambitions. He liked to be in the forefront of events, and actively

21

sought to be one step ahead of his fellows. He had arrived in Mombasa hoping to shoot the largest, rarest and most perfect specimens of game and was in a hurry to go upcountry, as he wanted to get there before too many other sportsmen spoilt the field.

A product of the late Victorian and Edwardian age, Northrup had the boundless enthusiasm and cheerful confidence typical of the era, as yet unscarred by the horrors of modern warfare. He had the rumbustious energy and brashness of a Strauss Waltz, the certain belief that his wealth and position would smooth his passage through life and an endless optimism that God was on his side. He was not a thinker, but a man of action, who revelled in nature and the outdoors life. He had life by the scruff of the neck and was determined to shake it until it yielded all he wanted from it. His attributes typify the period and Northrup was a man of his time.

The pioneering spirit of his forefathers had lodged deep in his soul and he wanted to emulate his ancestors and prove himself a worthy successor of those other adventurous Scottish McMillans who had crossed the seas to Canada and America. Both his father and his uncle, coming from humble beginnings, had built up successful businesses and became multi-millionaires. The son wished to make his mark in the world and show that he too could achieve great things, but so far all his projects had flopped. Northrup had the kind of restless energy, which drove him on, but left him unable to persevere for very long at anything. It was both his bad luck and good fortune, that he had no need to make a profit or achieve success. Overflowing with enthusiastic optimism, he lacked the spur of necessity, and the steel of determination that comes with it. But in British East Africa, he thought he had found a place where he could flourish and make his own mark. The country spoke to his inner man and he was spellbound and entranced by what he found.

He had come to shoot rhino and lion, but when he arrived at the foot of the small hump-like mountain Ol Donyo Sabuk, which rises unexpectedly from the flat grassland expanses of the Athi Plains, he refused to go further. The wildlife was prolific, the best shooting grounds he had seen in all his travels, the temperature was benign, and the scenery magnificent. The others of his party continued on, but he remained and bought 10,000 acres close to Ol Donyo Sabuk.

This is a tale of colonial Kenya, but with a slight twist. The central character is an American, an Anglophile, who supported the British Empire and its ideals. He became a pioneering and prominent settler, who sank much of his large fortune into the soil of his chosen country. After World War 1 he became involved in local politics, joining Lord Delamere in his fight for settler representation in government. After his death his wife built the McMillan library in his memory, a permanent reminder, which remains in Nairobi today, of a generous benefactor and true friend of Kenya. His town house, is today part of Nairobi University and Ol Donyo Sabuk, the mountain he loved so much, on which he is buried, is now a National Park.

> They that dig foundations deep
> Fit for realms to rise upon
> Little honour they reap
> Of their generation
> Any more than mountains gain
> Stature till we reach the plain

This verse from a poem written by Rudyard Kipling provides a fitting epitaph for many of those early Kenyan colonial settlers who never saw the fruits of their labours. It seems a particularly fitting one for Northrup who died in 1925, the same year Kipling wrote the poem.

During his lifetime, he seemed a failure. He frittered away his enormous fortune on over-ambitious projects and experiments, which came to nothing; his passions for hunting and wildlife were viewed as self-indulgent; his generosity a rich man's whim. The man was forgotten. Only his large size remembered – a disturbing symbol of colonial excess and power. Many years have now passed, and it is time that misconceptions are put to rest. The flat lands described in the poem have been reached; there is now enough distance between the plain and the mountain, for the story of an ardent American Anglophile and a pioneering settler in Kenya to be retold.

And now it only remains for me to offer my apologies for my blunt way of writing. I can only say in excuse for it that I am more accustomed to handle a rifle than a pen and cannot make any pretence to the grand literary flights and flourishes which I see in novels – for I sometimes like to read a novel. 'A sharp spear' runs the Kirkuana saying, 'needs no polish' and on the same principle I venture to hope that a true story, however strange it may be does not require to be decked out in fine words.

From Allan Quatermain's introduction to King Solomon's Mines, a source of fictional inspiration for Northrup and many others of his generation

CHAPTER I

SCOTTISH AND CANADIAN FORBEARS
AND AN AMERICAN UPBRINGING

William Northrup McMillan was the son of a multimillionaire, who made his fortune manufacturing railway freight trucks in St Louis, Missouri, USA. He came from a long line of other William McMillans who originated from Stranraer a port town in the south West of Scotland, which is nowadays the capital of the county of Dumfries and Galloway and a ferry port for Ireland. His ancestors were Scottish sea captains who traded to Philadelphia and Russia, bold and adventurous men who sailed the high seas in search of profit and lived dangerous lives.

Northrup's grandfather, another William McMillan (1810-74), emigrated from Scotland and settled in Canada in 1834. He and his wife Grace [1] had five sons – James, George, William, Hugh and John – and the Canadian census for 1861 lists them living in McNab Street south, in St Georges Ward, Hamilton, Ontario. Here grandfather William ran a grocery store and a tailoring shop and later supplied wood for the Great Western Railway. The Railway constructed in 1853 ran from Niagara to Hamilton and on to Windsor, Ontario, across the St Clair River from Detroit. This railway connection was to transform the lives of the McMillan family and it was with the railways in Detroit, that James the eldest son found his first position at the age of 16.

William McMillan (1842-1901), father of Northrup, was the third

---

1 Grace McMeaking (1811 -65) of Wigtown.

son. After leaving school at the age of 16 he became a clerk in a local hardware store. In 1864 he moved to Ingersoll, Ontario and opened his own hardware shop with his wife. He had married Eliza Northrup (1845-1915), daughter of George Northrup of Aylmer, Ontario, in 1863, when she was 18 and he just 21.[2] In 1868 William moved across the river into America and joined his elder brother James in Detroit, Michigan. James McMillan (1839 –1902) had made good and now had a flourishing business manufacturing railway rolling stock, called The Michigan Car and Foundry Company. In April 1870 his younger brother William, with help from James, opened up a branch factory in St Louis. This was known as the Missouri Car & Foundry Company and in a few short years was doing so well that William bought out his older brother. He became the sole owner in 1879.

The McMillan foundries were amongst the first to specialise in manufacturing railway trucks or freight cars, as they were generally

William McMillan, Northrup's father.   *Eliza McMillan, Northrup's mother.*

2 There are several alternative spellings for McMillan, McMillin and McMullen being two of the most common. This makes searching in archives for records especially challenging. The marriage record is listed under William McMillin. Later in life Northrup McMillan often styled himself MacMillan believing it a more authentic Scottish spelling.

known. To begin with these were made largely of wood but the McMillan foundries pioneered the use of steel and by the turn of the century almost all were made entirely of steel. The term car is rather misleading as of course there were no cars, or autos, as we know them today, and the cars made in the early McMillan foundries were boxes on wheels which ran on rails rather than roads. This was the great era of railway transport, and a period of expansion and wealth creation in America, which was eventually to make her the richest and most powerful nation in the world. A vast number of railroads were being built covering the continent from end to end and St Louis was a terminus for the railways going out West. There was a huge demand for goods trucks, or freight cars, and the McMillan brothers prospered greatly as a result.

William McMillan's factory in St Louis[3] could not cope with demand and a second was built in 1891 at Madison, Illinois. To give an idea of output, each of these factories produced 900 -1,000 freight cars monthly in addition to castings and general foundry output. By 1893 William employed more than 1600 men and his works in St Louis covered an area of over 25 acres. Besides the standard railway freight cars, he also produced box, flat, stock, refrigerator and caboose cars as well as all the wheels and brass bearings needed for the same.

The elder brother James, having made his fortune, moved out of manufacturing railway trucks and turned to politics and high finance[4], but William McMillan stuck to what he knew, churning out freight cars and box cars in ever increasing numbers from his factories. He was so successful that he began to acquire other foundry companies and in

3 The first plant was situated on five acres at 1401 North Main Street, St Louis. In 1875 this was moved to larger premises in East St Louis, but was burnt down in 1880 after a disastrous fire. After the fire the business was re-established in St Louis on the line of the Iron Mountain Railroad, between Ann and Dorcas Streets.
4 James McMillan entered the arena of politics in 1879 and was elected chairman of the Michigan Republican Party. In 1889 he was elected US senator (Class 2) from Michigan, a position he held until his death. The highest post he held while Senator was of Chairman of the Board of Manufactures. Despite no longer actively involved, he continued to take an interest in railway, shipbuilding and lake transportation companies and sat on the boards of several that were based in Detroit.

1899 came the biggest coup of all when headline reports for February 7th in the New York Times, announced that 'eight big car companies scattered over the United States have been combined under the name of American Car and Foundry Company'. Eventually the conglomerate would take over 18 formerly independent foundries to make a hugely successful giant company based in New York, which became known simply as ACF[5]. William McMillan sat on the Board of Directors as Chairman until his death.

This was the background into which the young Northrup was born and the environment in which he spent his formative years. The railway provided an ever-present leitmotiv throughout his life; his Scottish ancestry was a source of pride, while his Canadian parentage turned out to be surprisingly providential later on. Born 19th October 1872 in St Louis, he was sickly and undersized as an infant. His mother gave birth to three children – Mary, Percy and William Northrup – but only Northrup survived infancy. William and Eliza McMillan later gave donations for a women's university college at Washington University, St Louis, to be called Mary, in memory of the much-loved daughter they lost in infancy. Percy, who was not honoured with a memorial, was presumably a stillbirth. The birth and death dates of these children are not known, but they died before 1873, when they were re-interred in the McMillan Mausoleum in the Bellefontaine Cemetery. Northrup's birth, too, was unregistered, because in Missouri State before 1883 there was no provision for registration of births and deaths, and registration only became mandatory in 1910. The date and place of his birth however appears in his first passport dated 1890, when he is declared a citizen of the United States and gives the information that his father William McMillan had been naturalised as an American citizen before the circuit court in St Louis in 1874.

Very little is known about Northrup's early boyhood and the first definite mention of him comes in the US census for 1880. Here he is listed as living at 3004 Pine Street in St Louis City central, aged eight,

---

5 This company is still in existence today and trades under the name ACF Industries.

with his father and his mother.[6] This was a modest household, quite unlike the luxurious establishments he later became accustomed to. His father was listed as a car builder and his mother as a housewife.

Known as 'young Will,' as a boy, the first school he attended was a private preparatory day school in down town St Louis, called Smith Academy. This was situated on the corner of 19th Street and Washington Avenue, within easy walking distance from Pine Street, in a grim and forbidding building. The school took boys aged 6–11 and had 350 pupils. One contemporary recalled Will McMillan as a shy self-effacing lad[7]. This same classmate remembered the strict regime in school and how prepared lessons had to be learnt by heart and then recited aloud in class before the teacher. Lists of words had to be memorised with correct spelling and the boys were drilled for accuracy and speed in arithmetic. The dim gas-lit schoolroom had rows of wooden desks with inkwells and each class had up to 60 pupils. The shy and sickly Northrup did not do well in this environment.

With no organised sports such as football or baseball, the chief pastime of young boys in St Louis of that time was hunting, which young Will much preferred to schoolwork. Every boy had his gun and would explore the surrounding forests and pastures with a loaded, cocked shotgun over one shoulder or go duck shooting in the marshes of the Mississippi Missouri Rivers. The Cahokia Creek was a favourite spot for fishing, next to one of the Native Indian earthwork mounds, which were a feature of the St Louis area. Here the remains of an ancient civilisation could easily be collected as scattered bones and potsherds littered the ground.

In central St Louis there was plenty to catch the interest of a boy idling his time along the waterfront. On the river there was an endless stream of paddle steamers and laden barges churning up the muddy waters and blasting their whistles in warning. The great Eades Bridge spanned the river and carried long lines of rattling railway trucks out

---

6 They are listed in the census under the name McMellon, but appear in the city directories under McMillan.

7 Robert James Terry MD, "Memories of a long life in St Louis," *Bulletin of the Missouri Historical Society*, XII 2 (1956).

West and on the levees (landings) stevedores laboured unloading coal and pig iron for the factories and foundries. St Louis was not yet the enormous sprawling metropolis it has since become, but already it was a major transportation hub and gateway to the West, and the town was expanding rapidly as a centre for heavy industry.[8] Smoke belched from the factory chimneys covering the town in a sooty haze and everything was black with coal dust.

Although an only child, Northrup had no shortage of playmates to keep company with as he had great many cousins. The nearest were based at Michigan where Uncle James and his wife had six children – William, Charles, Grace Fisher, James Howard, Amy, Philip Hamilton and Francis Wetmore. Amy and Philip Hamilton were the two closest in age to Northrup. Uncle Hugh, William's younger brother, also lived in Detroit and had a large brood of children[9]. Northrup's mother Eliza by all accounts was outgoing and generous by nature, and liked to have young people around her, making up for the loss of her own children. Northrup's father, William, was a quiet man, only interested in his work.

Northrup received his secondary education at The Hill School, Pottstown, Pennsylvania. The humid and polluted air of St Louis affected his weak chest badly and he later referred to the 'beastly climate of St Louis'[10]so it was likely for reasons of health as well as for education that his parents sent him to this small family boarding school, away from the rough and tumble of city life.

---

8 Today St Louis is in decline as the old means of transport have been superseded by road and air. The grand buildings in the town centre are often empty and there is low employment.

9 Hugh McMillan (1845-1907) had joined his eldest brother James in Detroit immediately after leaving school at the age of 16 and worked in the Union Trust Bank. He was not as successful as his brothers, but produced a number of hopeful daughters.

10 St Louis has an extreme climate, with hot humid summers and very cold winters. The dampness from the rivers and marshes and the smoke from the chimneys combined to cover downtown St Louis in a permanent haze, which is often captured in the paintings and photographs of the period.

The choice of The Hill School, Pottstown, Pennsylvania[11], was interesting. It was founded in 1851 as a 'Family Boarding School for boys and young men,' by the Rev Matthew Meigs. The idea was that students boarded and lived under a surrogate family rule. The major aim was the inculcation of Christian morality and doctrine and continuous personal supervision of the child's whole growth, which the founder believed could best be accomplished in a relatively isolated community. The school was not modelled on English prototypes but rather on Swiss and German boarding schools considered the most enlightened and progressive at the time. It aimed to have a curriculum flexible enough to shape a programme for each boy according to his own future business. Initially no diplomas were given; a boy could stay for the length of time his parents wanted or needed. A thorough education to the limit of a boy's ability was offered but more important was character development. Discipline was maintained by appeals to heart and conscience rather than the fear of punishment.

The earliest pictures of the school show an elegant two-storey building surrounded by a veranda set up on a hill; the grounds are landscaped and a long, sloping driveway leads up to the entrance. Inside the main hall, over the fireplace, was carved a quote from St Paul – 'Add to your Faith, Virtue and to Virtue, Knowledge' – words which exactly summed up the educational ethos of the school. The walls were panelled with wood and the spacious dormitories had solid oak furniture.

By the time Northrup went to The Hill, John Meigs, son of the founder Reverend Meigs, was headmaster and the curriculum was becoming more structured. Three courses were offered: classical, scientific and business. Presumably Northrup was enrolled for the business course. The school took boys aged 10-18. In 1884 there were 59 students, but this had risen to 101 in 1889, with 17 faculty members. John Meigs was a very successful head and during his tenure the school underwent considerable expansion despite two devastating fires, which burnt down the new gymnasium and classrooms. Based in

11 Paul Chancellor, *The History of The Hill School 1851-1976*, (1976). School motto: 'Whatsoever Things Are True.'

the countryside just outside Pottstown, which was a centre for iron and steel manufacture, the boys were removed from the distractions and supposed corruption of urban life.

In the School history, it is stated that truth was the School's highest ideal. The five most important character qualities, which were to be developed in young men, were: obedience, truthfulness, purity, unselfishness and service. Athletics and sport and a strong Christian code were emphasised and music was encouraged with plenty of singing in the chapel. The idea of purity was promoted with a prime example being King Arthur's knight Sir Galahad: "whose strength was at the strength of ten because his heart was pure." During Northrup's time at school a cadet corps, a uniformed military unit, was formed and the boys drilled four times a week. There was a rifle club as well, where the boys learnt to shoot.

The older boys were expected to help the younger ones and the family concept was encouraged and can be seen in the 1888 school photo where pupils and teachers are seen mingling in a charmingly casual way. Northrup McMillan may well be there amongst them. He would have been about 15 or 16 at the time, a gangly dark haired and dark eyed teenager. Sadly, due to another fire in 1973, all school records prior to that date were lost, so it is not known for how many years Northrup attended the Hill, nor what kind of pupil he was – but presumably he was not a good one as he did not succeed in graduating![12]

Was it his mother who chose the school? She was artistic and interested in the education of the young and she would have approved of the Christian ideals. Perhaps she was anxious about his health and thought that the hill top position of the school and cool, fresh air of Pennsylvania would be beneficial. Or was it his father? The Presbyterian and Scottish background of the headmaster and structured routine would have appealed to McMillan senior. Boarding schools were rare

12 The only surviving record of Northrup's attendance (a list of old boys who fought in WWI) gives a date of 1893x, showing that he left without graduating. In 1893 he would have been 21, rather too old for school, so one can only suppose that his place was kept open until 1893, in case he wished to return and take his final exams.

in the United States, unlike in England, where the public school system was well established.

Northrup was not academically inclined and seems always to have preferred the outdoor life and nature to the schoolroom, let alone the factories and foundries of his father. As a teenager he wanted to be an explorer or a cowboy, not a railroad baron. His father William McMillan was a self-made millionaire, his uncle a US Senator – hard working, high achievers and a hard act to follow. Possibly his cousins went to the same school or perhaps his parents may have hoped the rigorous discipline and routine of a boarding school would lead to a well rounded individual and an improvement in the character and health of their only son.

Scholastic studies aside, another reason for educating a son at a good boarding school was to provide opportunities lacking in the family environment. The McMillans had sprung from relatively humble origins and were described as unpretentious. Probably they hoped that their son would learn to become a 'gentleman,' mixing with other sons of wealthy, influential and well-born parents. Although America was not as tainted as Europe by a class system, manners and social graces backed by wealth were much admired and greased the hinges of many doors.

There is no doubt that his time at the school left a lasting impression on Northrup and elements of his training there re-occur throughout his life. The scrupulous attention to correct dress, manners and etiquette demanded at The Hill remained with him. His courtly manners were often commented upon in later life and gave him a useful entrée into Society. He enjoyed the boys alone, chummy life style of boarding school and tried to recreate it in his African ranch. His experience of life at boarding school helped him get along with the English public school boys he met later on in Europe and Kenya, as he understood their fondness for sport and boyish pranks. The idea of service and helping those less fortunate also seems to have rubbed off, certainly in later life. However, the puritanical self discipline and rigorous living encouraged at school was not carried through; his nature, though kindly and generous, was fundamentally self indulgent.

Like his father and uncles before him, Northrup probably left school at 16 in 1888, to join his father in the freight car business. At this age he was a clumsy, and not overly intelligent youth with no skill with words or the pen[13], who must have found working with his strict and silent father an intimidating and uncomfortable experience. A late developer who had been undersized as a boy, he was now shooting up rapidly and outgrowing his strength.

At the factory his father William had a new and exceptionally talented assistant called William Keeney Bixby, who could do no wrong and had established himself as the boss's favourite. William Keeney Bixby (1857-1931) had originally worked as night watchman and baggage-man for the International Great Northern Railroad at Palestine, Texas, but his intelligence and pleasant manner brought him to the attention of the owner who gave him quick promotion to general baggage agent in San Antonio. From there Bixby moved to St Louis and was taken on by William McMillan, president of the Missouri Car and Foundry Company. After only one year working for William McMillan, Bixby was promoted to Vice President and General Manager at the early age of 31 in 1888. This swift promotion was attributed to his successful and skilful renegotiation of a disastrous contract his employer had made for the purchase of pig iron, which is an essential

William Keeney Bixby, Northrup's father's right hand man and business partner.

---

13 The only McMillan handwritten letters to survive are telegrams or short notes consisting of a few hastily scrawled words. Longer letters and business letters are always typed by a secretary with just a quick signature at the bottom - W N McMillan. Even the signature was sometimes written by someone else. It seems that he very rarely ever put pen to paper.

ingredient in steel production. The good relations Bixby managed to make with the pig iron supplier rescued the company from a loss-making situation and demonstrated the extraordinary business talent of his assistant. It is tempting to speculate that the disastrous contract was actually made by Northrup, who had just joined his father in business. Perhaps it was after this that William McMillan took the decision that his son was not ready for a responsible managerial position and led him to promote Bixby instead. William senior came to rely upon Bixby more and more as he stepped down from the day-to-day running of his factories, due to a heart condition, and Bixby became his trusted right hand man and business partner.

What kind of relationship there was between Bixby and Northrup at this period is not known. They certainly knew each other well, but there was a fifteen-year age gap, so it was unlikely that their friendship was close. It is easy to imagine that Northrup might have felt some resentment or jealousy, as it was William Keeney Bixby who received the father's approval and praise, and inherited the mantle of the father rather than the son. Bixby had all the attributes of a successful businessman, while Northrup did not.

What is certain is that Northrup did not enjoy working with his father and Bixby and he actively disliked the environment of factories and foundries. He did not thrive and his health began to suffer. In 1890 he contracted a serious bronchial infection, which his parents feared was the onset of consumption (tuberculosis) and they decided to send him to the dry climate of New Mexico to regain his health.

CHAPTER II

LIFE WITH THE COWBOYS AND DREAMS OF AFRICA

Northrup remained in New Mexico for three years to recover his health, which he did and on his return in 1893 he weighed 250 pounds and stood 6 feet 3 inches tall. The 'bronchial infection' was possibly the early signs of TB (tuberculosis), which was prevalent at the time or it could have been an acute bout of bronchial asthma, as chest infections were particularly common in St Louis.[14] The clinical stage of TB often appeared in young people as they approached adulthood, when they put on a spurt of growth and outgrew their strength. Northrup was aged 17/18 in 1890 and had just grown an unusual amount. Whatever his underlying condition was, his illness must have been severe and in the pre-antibiotic age, when there was no certain cure for infections, a cause of great anxiety for his parents as they took the drastic step of sending him away to recover his health. In 1882 a breakthrough had been made when a German scientist Robert Koch discovered the bacillus responsible for tuberculosis. Sanatoriums began to be set up to isolate the sufferers and treat them. The medically approved regimen consisted of

14 Dr Pascal James Imperato, Dean and distinguished Service Professor of the School of Public Health, State University of New York, personal interview.

nutritious food, fresh air and rest, preferably in a high, dry and sunny place. New Mexico, with its high elevation, abundant sunshine and dry climate, was considered ideal. Thousands of people flocked to New Mexico from 1880 through 1940 seeking a cure for tuberculosis and other diseases affecting the lungs.

Treatments varied. At Fort Stanton patients were required to stay outdoors at least eight hours daily and always had to keep the windows open when indoors. Patients at Santa Fe's Sunmount Sanatorium stayed in special cottages equipped with screened sleeping porches. Rest, in fact, was a key element of the treatment. Patients were advised to sleep at least ten hours at night and spend another seven hours during the day resting. Eating well was another key element of the cure; this meant three good square meals a day, with milk taken between meals. Six glasses of milk a day were recommended at the start of treatment and weight gain was considered an important indicator of progress. A positive optimistic frame of mind was encouraged and sanatoriums often sponsored concerts, lectures, horseback rides and excursions to nearby pueblos for the patients. It was firmly believed that a cheerful and hopeful spirit had an influence over the processes of the body.

Sanatoriums were expensive; they cost about $100 a month, (a lot of money in those days) especially as the average treatment lasted nine months. Northrup was fortunate that his parents could afford the costs of medical treatment and he stayed in New Mexico nearly three years trying to rid himself of his symptoms. No record remains of exactly where he was in New Mexico, or whether indeed he attended a sanatorium or was treated privately at his parent's property. The experience, however, made a deep impression on Northrup and influenced his subsequent life style. He was always very careful of his health. His overeating habit, which was to lead to serious obesity in later life, was perhaps also a result of the treatment, as was his aversion to exercise of any kind – although strenuous activity may have exacerbated his asthma. On the positive side, his often noted optimism and cheerfulness may have been learnt while under doctor's orders in New Mexico, and for the rest of his life he sought out fresh air and open spaces preferably at a high elevation, with a sunny dry climate.

Whether or not Northrup suffered from bronchial asthma is hard to say for certain, although there are various indications that he probably did. Interestingly, treatment for asthmatics at this time included asthma cigarettes, often made from patented herbs, but ordinary tobacco was also thought to be beneficial. Northrup was a heavy smoker, and he often appears in photographs holding a cigarette. On safari he always carried a little pouch of cigarettes attached to his belt.

It is unlikely Northrup did much active ranching while in New Mexico, though his time spent in contact with cowboys gave him a life long appreciation of the 'Wild West.' In her book *Red Strangers*, C S Nicholls writes that Northrup would often lapse into a broad Texan accent when his wife, Lucie, was not around. Lucie, who spoke with barely a trace of an American accent, did not approve of cowboys or their manners and his speech would abruptly change when she came into the room.[15]

According to a newspaper report, it was during his time in New Mexico that 'he learnt to ride, rope and above all shoot without taking aim as is the quick western way.'[16] He gained his love of hunting and developed a taste for the outdoor life from the cowboys and afterwards 'was never content until he had hidden himself in some country far away from civilisation.' His stay in New Mexico reinforced his boyhood preferences.

In the late 19th century the written word was the main media for disseminating ideas amongst a wide audience and, besides his own experiences, Northrup drew inspiration from the books he read. The 'Boys Own' atmosphere of his boarding school would almost certainly have been reinforced by reading of certain texts and reading was one of the few things he could do during his convalescence in New Mexico. Books about real life heroes featured large in the late Victorian era,

15 C S Nicholls, *Red Strangers: The White Tribe of Kenya* (2005), 59.
16 W N McMillan Scrapbooks RH, Micr.Afr.641. The newspaper cuttings in the two scrapbooks are stuck in somewhat randomly and often do not include the date or the name of the newspaper – this article is probably from the *St Louis Globe*.

and it was a handful of these larger than life figures, who shaped the young Northrup's dreams for his future.

Interest in explorers and African adventurers had reached an all time peak and one of the most glamorous was the British hunter-explorer Frederick Courteney Selous (1851-1917). His trailblazing book, *A Hunters Wanderings in Africa,* first published in 1881, went into several editions and made 'big game hunting' and adventurous exploration in Africa fashionable. Northrup would have read the book at about the age of 14 or 15, when a boy is at his most impressionable, and Selous became his life-long hero and later his friend. Selous' book starts with a description how the author at the age of 19 with £400 in his pocket first set foot in Africa determined to become an explorer and adopt a life of ever-varying scenes and excitement. With no exact plan in his head, but an optimistic belief in himself, he heads for the Diamond Fields and the story of his nine years wanderings in Africa unfolds. Told in straightforward language, the book is easy to read, with a good amount of suspense and excitement. It is full of interesting facts about the natural world and has plenty of illustrations. Striking just the right note, the book quickly became a best seller on both sides of the Atlantic.

Selous' second book, *Travel and Adventure in South East Africa*, published 1893, when Northrup was about 21, describes an expedition to collect specimens for museums in England. With its terrifying accounts of meetings with wild animals and illustrations of outsize lions with manes

Frederick Courteney Selous as a young man in hunting costume. He is wearing shorts and his characteristic floppy hat is lying at his feet.

bristling and teeth bared, the book thrilled the imaginations of many young men eager for danger and excitement and ensured the author's lasting fame.[17]

Selous' real-life adventures inspired the writer Rider Haggard to create the fictional Allan Quatermain character.[18] Haggard's novels of African adventures[19] were another best-selling sensation of the period and Northrup would certainly have read them.

Selous was an iconic figure to many young men of Northrup's generation – a cross between a pop star and a sports celebrity. They copied his style of casual wear, open necked shirt with sleeves rolled up, a handkerchief knotted carelessly about the neck and a floppy wide brimmed, double terai slouch hat on the head. They wanted to experience the thrills of 'African Big Game Hunting' and fantasised about becoming famous explorers.

Northrup hero-worshipped Selous more than most. Northrup

---

17 Born in London to a wealthy family of French-Huguenot extraction, his father was at one time chairman of the London Stock Exchange. From an early age Selous showed a deep interest in the outdoors and wildlife and was drawn by stories of explorers and their adventures and was determined to follow in their footsteps. His parents hoped he would become a doctor, but his love for natural history made him want to study the ways of wild animals in their native habitat. Going to South Africa at age of 19, he spent nine years hunting and exploring the little known regions north of the Transvaal and south of the Congo Basin. His travels added greatly to the knowledge of the country now called Zimbabwe. In 1890 at the request of Cecil Rhodes, he entered the service of the British South Africa Company and was part of the pioneer expedition to Mashonaland. He fought and was wounded in the first Matabele War 1893. In the same year he married Marie Maddy, with whom he had two sons. In later life he became a conservationist as he realised how the impact of European hunters was leading to a significant reduction in the wild animal population in Africa. He was much in demand for organising and leading hunting expeditions and was considered the foremost expert on African game. He donated animal and plant specimens to the Natural History Museum in South Kensington, London and his bust, put there in 1920, stands there still.

18 The adventures of his brother Jack Haggard, first vice-consul in Lamu, also provided material for his books.

19 *King Solomon's Mines* (1885), *Allan Quatermain* (1887) and *She* (1887) were the most popular titles.

wanted to go to Africa and shoot a lion, but his father did not approve and thought the whole idea dangerous nonsense. But Northrup persisted with his dream. At the earliest opportunity, after his father's death, he went to Africa on a hunting expedition, even collected specimens for British museums, just like Selous. In 1909 when Theodore Roosevelt, the ex-president of the United States, was staying with Northrup at his game lodge in Kenya, Northrup left his illustrious guest in order to go on a hunting trip with Selous. When Selous was killed in World War I, Northrup was devastated. He mourned his hero and gave generous donations to the Selous Memorial Fund.

To his contemporaries Selous represented the ideal combination of a perfect English Gentleman and a Wild West Cowboy. He was a fine sportsman, but modest about his achievements, intelligent, but not overtly so. He was a handsome man, with a strong physique and distinguished bearing, clear blue eyes and a magnetic personality, which made him unforgettable to those who met him.

Hunting was considered a manly pastime. It was a dangerous, adrenaline sport, attracting young men, who perhaps nowadays would go in for motor racing or stunt flying. It was considered good training for those who intended to become leaders of men and empire builders and was actively encouraged by public figures such as Theodore Roosevelt, president of America.[20] Successful hunters were idolised as role models. Lion hunting in Africa was an even more exotic and extreme form of the sport making it doubly attractive and fascinating.

Another African explorer who Northrup would have certainly known about was Henry Morton Stanley, of 'Dr Livingstone, I presume!' fame. H M Stanley's life history was a classic rags to riches tale and his exploits were well known by every self-respecting schoolboy. Abandoned by his mother to a workhouse in Wales, Stanley jumped ship in New Orleans in 1859, fought in the American Civil War, became a journalist and led an expedition to central Africa to find the missionary David Livingstone. Stanley ended up the most successful

---

20 Theodore Roosevelt, *The Wilderness Hunter* (1893) gives an account of the Big Game in the US and its chase with horse, hound and rifle. The grizzly bear and the bison or buffalo were the largest animals hunted.

and ruthless explorer of his age, married a society heiress and was showered with honours.

In 1890 Stanley went on a six-month lecture tour of the United States and it's quite possible Northrup attended one of his well-publicised talks about his adventures in Africa. Stanley travelled throughout America from coast to coast and from Canada to Texas, in a private railway carriage, a Pullman coach named 'The Henry M Stanley.' It was luxuriously fitted out with kitchen, bathroom, three bedrooms and an observation platform, and stopped at every station, where he was scheduled to give one of his talks. He was lionised wherever he went and the tour was an enormous success with the American public.

Closer to home was yet another influential figure and school boy hero. This was William Frederik Cody, better known as Buffalo Bill. Buffalo Bill was one of the most colourful figures of the American West. His Wild West shows glamorised the adventurous life of the cowboy and thrilled a whole generation of schoolboys and many adults too. His circus-like shows featured daring horseback riding, spinning lasso displays and dramatic re-enactments such as Red Indian attacks on wagon trains, or stagecoach robberies. Sitting Bull, a real life Indian chief with an entourage of twenty braves would come on stage in full regalia. The female stars, Annie Oakley and Calamity Jane would demonstrate their quick draw shooting abilities and as a popular finale, Cody would ride in with an entourage of cowboys to defend a settler family from a band of Indians. The show was a sensation. It was so popular that in 1887 he was asked to perform in front of Queen Victoria at her Golden Jubilee. Buffalo Bill brought his whole troupe to England and then toured Europe for a further six months. The effect a live enactment must have had on the romantic imagination of a schoolboy cannot be underestimated.

Buffalo Bill got his nickname after he undertook a contract to supply the Kansas Pacific Railroad workers with buffalo meat. To fulfil his contract he killed 4,280 buffalo, in eight months, between 1867 and 1868. This was the era of the Wild West with open plains teeming with buffalo and other wild animals, an unspoilt, untouched wilderness full of opportunities and dangers for the adventurous pioneer. By the 1890s all that had changed with the railway bringing settlers and commerce, the ranch lands fenced off for farms, while the Native Indian tribes were confined to reservations. Young Northrup would have to look elsewhere to find another playground to satisfy his romantic hankerings for the Wild West and somewhere else to carve out his own individual niche.

In 1893 Northrup was considered well enough to return to St Louis and for the next five years until 1898 he behaved as a dutiful son and worked for his father and was based in St. Louis and was given the nominal position of assistant general manager. However, car foundries held little attraction for him. Northrup worked there reluctantly and continued to dream of exploration and big game hunting in Africa.

By this time the McMillans had moved from central St Louis to a new leafy suburb on the west side of town close to a spacious open area called Forest Park. Here they lived in an imposing mansion, built in the classical Italian Renaissance style, at number 25 Portland Place. The house had been commissioned by the McMillans and was constructed in 1892. It was designed by the architects Eames and Young and still

25 Portland Place, St Louis, the imposing mansion built for the McMillans in 1892 in classical Italian Resaissance style. It still stands in all its grandeur today.

stands in all its grandeur today. It is has a portico entrance, decorative swags on the façade, a balustrade along the top and large windows. The garden and house used to be enclosed behind iron railings, which must have given it a somewhat forbidding aspect, but these have since been removed. For some reason Northrup particularly disliked the house. Here his mother Eliza, or Aunt Lizzie, as she was known in the family circle, surrounded herself with numerous nieces and nephews, who came to stay for extended periods. When not entertaining at home, or worshipping at the First Presbyterian Church of which she was

an enthusiastic parishioner, Eliza occupied herself with charitable works and visited her large circle of friends.

Soon after his return from New Mexico, at the age of 22 Northrup married Lucie Webber in 1894 in Leon, Florida. He had first met her in St Louis, where she had lived as a young girl, but they met up again in Paris (possibly when Northrup was on a business trip) and decided to marry.

Lucie Fairbanks Webber of Northampton Massachusetts was born 26th June 1867 in St Johnsbury, Caledonia, Vermont, and died in Kenya, September 1957. She was

William Northrup McMillan married Lucie Webber in 1894 in Leon, Florida.

five years older than Northrup. Her father was a clergyman, George N Webber DD (1826-95) and her mother was Charlotte Fairbanks (1837-1869). Lucie was the youngest child of four. The oldest daughter Agnes, born in 1860, died at the age of three, but two other siblings survived: Annie born in 1863 and Frederick Fairbanks Webber born in 1865. Lucie is described in a passport application for 1887, when she was living in Berlin, as 5 feet 5 inches tall with brown eyes and brown hair.

Her father remarried after her mother's death and had further children from his second marriage.

George Webber, her father, had been a professor of metaphysics in Amherst College Massachusetts for a while, but he resigned in 1854, when he then took holy orders. He seems to have been a restless soul, who travelled a good deal and appears under several different addresses in USA. Lucie's grandfather on the maternal side, Thaddeus Fairbanks (1796-1886), was an inventor. He invented the platform scale and held 32 patents on scales as well as many other patents for inventions.

Lucie Fairbanks Webber was clever, musical and artistic, slim and sophisticated, all things that her future husband was not, and even her friends were surprised at her choice of husband.[21] It seems to have been an attraction of opposites or possibly even a marriage of convenience. They were married quietly and informally at the Webber house in Leon, Florida, and no report of their marriage appeared in the local newspapers. One rather unromantic anecdote survives of their wedding day. Just before the marriage ceremony Northrup had engaged in a game of billiards in the bride's home. Lucie interrupted the game with the news that the minister had arrived to marry them.

"Wait till I wash my hands and put on my coat," he said.

"Never mind that!" was her answer. "Just come up and be married," and according to friends, that is just what he did.[22]

As the daughter of a clergyman and presumably not particularly well off, Northrup was a catch for her, but the McMillan family may have hoped for someone better born, prettier and younger. Marriage

---

21 "Long before Miss Lucie Webber of Northampton, Mass., married she was recognised as an extraordinary girl. A young woman of many talents, an artist, a capable writer and a gifted musician, she preferred her books and her art to the social diversions to which girls devoted most of their time. She went to Paris to complete her musical education and instead met and wed a St Louis millionaire. Her friends in society were somewhat surprised. They had expected that she would do something that would be very much out of the ordinary and they were a little disappointed to think that she probably would lead the comparatively commonplace existence of a rich man's wife." (Annette Gordon (1909) W N McMillan Scrapbooks RH,Micr.Afr.641).
22 *St Louis Post-Dispatch*, 29 March 1925.

gave Northrup the opportunity to live an independent life away from the parental home. For the first few years the young couple lived in St Louis, at 3700 Delmar Boulevard. A new mansion at 21 Washington Terrace, close to the family home at Portland Place, was built for them in 1898 in the fashionable French chateau style but they never occupied it.[23]

In 1898 Northrup and Lucie moved to England. Here Northrup was employed until 1901 as Europe Representative for the American Car and Foundry Co. There was considerable trade with England and Europe by this time and the Berwick Plant of ACF supplied rolling stock for the new London Underground. Unfortunately, the records for the Missouri Company and the early years of ACF have been lost, so we do not know exactly what Northrup did – probably not much! A clue to his life in England is found in the 1901 census for Great Britain, which records him as living with his wife in Finchley, Middlesex, on the outskirts of London. In this he lists his profession as Contracting Engineer. He is the head of a substantial household with 20 servants, including butler, footman, maids and gardeners. Two American guests are also listed, Grace Fisher (his cousin) and a friend.

Contracting Engineer is a vague term and it is likely that he acted as an overseas Public Relations man, meeting with customers, and making contacts, which could be useful for future business. In another passport application, Northrup describes himself as an export agent. With his sociable nature and polished manners – when he chose – this was an area in which he could be successful. Without his father and Bixby breathing down his neck at every turn, Northrup found his feet and became his own man. There is no doubt he enjoyed living in Edwardian London, for he kept a house there for the rest of his life, while he did not enjoy living in St Louis.

Since no records survive, it is difficult to know what kind of relationship Northrup had with his parents, but it was evidently not a happy one. It is significant that he spent a large part of his early life either at boarding school or recovering in New Mexico, far from the

---

23 The façade for the house was closely based on a hotel in Paris.

family home and this set a pattern for his later life. It appears that though his mother lavished care and attention on those less fortunate in life and had many friends, her relationship with her only surviving child was poor. Her smothering love and over-anxious concern for his health drove him away.

Amongst the Bixby papers housed in the Missouri History Museum Research Library is a telling interview. As an old man Bixby was asked the secret to success in life. Was it to have rich parents who could give you a start and a job? No, said Bixby. He said he felt sorry for the rich man's son, when the mother interferes and worries for dear Willie's health as she fears he is working too long at the factory and persuades the father that his boy's health is more important than the job being done, or coming in on time.

Northrup's father, who favoured his employee Bixby over his son, was a workaholic, totally committed to his business interests. He had the reputation of being an exacting employer, who had no time for incompetence, or slackness in the workplace. It was said that the Scotch Covenanter was strong in him. He despised show, scorned ostentation, and was blunt and to the point in speech. His imperious manner hid a kind heart, but he had little sympathy or understanding for his son. Parenting of course was very different in the 19th century and it is dangerous to make comparisons with expectations of today,

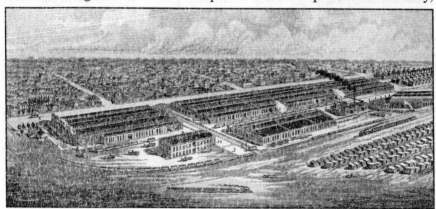

A bird's eye view of the American Car & Foundry Plant in St Louis. The industry started by Northrup's father was the source of the family wealth.

but Northrup does not seem to have enjoyed a happy relationship with either of his parents. The spectres of the dead siblings hung heavy in the household and no doubt they were disappointed in their failure to have other children and in the health and ability of the child that survived. Northrup grew to resent the ties of duty and the burden of expectation and turned to other role models to give him the guidance he wanted. He rejected the foundries and factories of his father and left his hometown as soon as the opportunity arose.

On November 15th 1901, William McMillan died of heart failure and pneumonia at his house in St Louis. Northrup was summoned home from England and arrived just in time to see his father before he died. Shortly before death he had given a generous bequest to Washington University in St Louis to build a women's college, to be called the Mary Institute. Both William and Eliza were keen supporters of education for women and after her husband's death she made further bequests to the university for a dormitory for women students, which was called the McMillan hall as a memorial to her husband.[24]

Bixby was made the chief executor of the McMillan will. His fortune, estimated at nearly seven million dollars, was left equally divided between his wife and son. Bixby was one of the main mourners at the funeral and in his tribute he described William McMillan as an unusual man, who was modest and retiring in private life, but forceful and enterprising in business – a man who liked to deal with great enterprises and loved work for its own sake, but did not especially value for himself the large fortune he acquired. Bixby said that William McMillan's greatest pleasure came from helping others and he was an early proponent of women's education because he foresaw the importance of women in the changing social economic conditions of the age.

---

24 The McMillan Hall was opened in 1907.

CHAPTER III

AFRICA AT LAST!

THE FIRST LION HUNT AND EXPEDITION TO THE BLUE NILE

After the death of Northrup's father, the young couple's life changed radically. Northrup, now aged 29, inherited a large fortune, and money seemed to beget money. Funds he invested in the Ploesti oil fields in Roumania and Malayan rubber, gave extraordinarily good returns. He was an extremely wealthy young man, who no longer had any need to follow a profession or to prove himself to his father. He was free to do whatever he wanted to do and that's exactly what he did. With Bixby in St Louis looking after the company and the financial side of things, his mother immersed in her charitable work and her wide circle of friends, without children or siblings to provide for, Northrup found himself with a large amount of money that was entirely his to spend as he thought fit.

And what did he think fit? According to his obituary in the East African Standard:

"The fascination of big game hunting and the exploration of Africa attracted him and for the next four years he followed his inclination in that direction and travelled extensively."

Immediately following his father's death Northrup took Lucie to Cairo to see the pyramids and the Sahara desert. But on hearing there was excellent hunting to be had in Ethiopia, he left his wife with friends, who were going back to Europe, and went in search of lions. He travelled from Cairo to Port Said and from there to Jibuti. At Jibuti he recruited the best porters money could buy and all the personnel needed for a hunting trip, totalling more than fifty men.[25] Accompanied by a friend, Frank Case[26], the two young men set off in high spirits towards the Ethiopian border, eager for adventure and the thrill of lion hunting. It is easy to imagine how, released from the fetters of filial obedience, Northrup looked forward to the trip with excited anticipation. It had long been his dream to visit Africa and shoot a lion, and now at last the opportunity had come. But as with many African adventures, delays and obstacles had to be overcome and unexpected dangers lurked in the wings.

At one point their caravan was besieged by a band of Mahdist warriors returning to the Coast, swathed in white robes and bristling with weaponry. After some anxious moments, their leader and Northrup agreed to negotiate and, as recalled by Northrup, being unable to communicate in any other way, the two men sat down and eyeballed each other. Northrup out stared his opponent and the travellers continued on their separate ways, in peace.

Then they were delayed as they waited for permission from Ras Mkonnen[27], governor of Harar, to enter Ethiopia and hunt lion in his

---

25 Several of the personnel he recruited on this first expedition worked for him again and were then employed permanently by him when he settled in Kenya. Northrup was a generous employer and staff tended to remain with him.
26 Possibly the same Frank Case who founded the famous Algonquin Hotel in New York and was a writer. They probably met in the famous and luxurious Shepheards Hotel in Cairo, where Northrup always stayed whenever he was in Cairo.
27 Makonnen Wolde Mikael Gudessa (1852-1906) usually known as Ras Makonnen was made governor of Harar in 1887. He was first cousin to emperor Menelik II and acted as his de facto foreign minister. He died unexpectedly of typhus in 1906 aged 53. His son known at this stage as Tafari Makonnen (1892-1975) would eventually become emperor Haile Selassie.

territory. To kill time and keep the men occupied and out of mischief during this enforced period of inactivity, Northrup organised running, jumping and wrestling matches, and shooting demonstrations. What happened next is not entirely clear as the information has to be gleaned from fireside stories, reported many years later, which tended to be embellished – but events went roughly as follows: Understandably, Northrup, was finding the long wait frustrating. The Ethiopian border officials were harassing his men, demanding money and generally being obstructive. There was no sign of the hunting permit or a border pass. Northrup could stand it no longer. He refused to take no for an answer, lost his temper and punched one haughty official on the nose. The Ethiopian fell like a stone to the ground knocked unconscious by the blow, bleeding copiously from ears and mouth. News of this audacious treatment of his official reached the ears of Ras Mkonnen and, fortunately for Northrup, he took it in good part and expressed a wish to meet the American hunters. Northrup was given an audience and when he presented the Ras with a gun and treated him to a shooting display of quick firing in the Wild West cowboy fashion, success was a forgone conclusion. The Ethiopians had never met men from America before or seen a gun twirled in the hand and fired with such rapidity and accuracy at the target. They were used to Frenchmen with rifles, which needed slow and careful aim. They were most impressed. Ras Mkonnen and Northrup became firm friends and the hunting permit was granted.

Northrup with his entry pass and permit in hand set off immediately in search of lions. On this occasion he killed three lions, but his first lion kill was by far the most exciting and the one he liked to recall and retell around the evening campfire. The iron nerve required and narrow escape from injury made it an experience to rival those of a Selous or Alan Quatermain! Northrup, his beaters and his two gun bearers surprised a large lion lying in undergrowth. Northrup's initial shot went into the lion's jaw, knocking out one of his teeth, and the startled and enraged animal sprang at him. Northrup's faithful gunbearer coolly handed him a second gun and while the lion was in the air, he shot at it, the western way without sighting, and the bullet hit the beast under the foreleg going through to the heart. The lion fell dead almost at his feet. That night there was great rejoicing in camp. The Christians drank brandy and all night long there was the sound of revelry and much chanting of songs and Northrup was feted as a great and mighty hunter.[28]

This trip filled Northrup with a desire for further African adventures and on his return to England he set about organising a more ambitious and elaborate expedition to Ethiopia.

In the introduction to his book '*W N McMillan's Expeditions and Big-game Hunting in Sudan, Abyssinia and British East Africa*'; written by Burchart Heinrich Jessen in 1906, Jessen stated that Mr McMillan first went to Ethiopia in 1902 to recuperate his health but made no mention of his father's death or the exciting hunting trip, which followed. Commissioned by Northrup McMillan and for private distribution only (the height of chic at this period) the book provides an invaluable source of information for the next four years of Northrup's life. By no stretch of imagination, could Abyssinia (or Ethiopia as it was more properly called) be considered a usual health spa destination. So what, besides the climate, altitude, and wildlife, prompted Northrup's interest in this remote African empire?

By 1902 the railway line from Jibuti up to Dire Dawa was running, but as yet was not connected to Addis Ababa, the now capital of Ethiopia. The French-built railway was unreliable and the engines kept breaking down and stopping on the steep climb. Having reached Dire Dawa, it then took 14 days hard climbing to reach the Ethiopian capital. Northrup had the idea of trying out a different, more direct route. He wanted to see if it was possible to travel by river from Ethiopia through to Khartoum in Anglo-Egyptian Sudan. From Khartoum transportation links to Egypt and the rest of the world were good thanks to the Sudan Express Railway and the Nile steamers. It was known that the source of the Blue Nile was in Lake Tana in the north of Ethiopia, but the river itself had never been fully explored as no-one as yet had managed

---

28 W N McMillan Scrapbooks RH, Micr.Afr.641.

to run the rapids and negotiate the cataracts. It seemed a perfect venture, daring and timely. It was an ambitious project, but in 1902 and 1903 conditions were uniquely favourable.

The whole region of Egypt, Sudan and Ethiopia was enormously high profile at this period. There was the fascination with General Gordon, who had died at Khartoum, killed by the Mahdi's army. His death had been avenged by the recent successes of General Kitchener, who in 1898 had defeated the Islamic army of the Mahdists at Omdurman. The day-to-day detail of Kitchener's successful military expedition up the Nile had been brought to life by the popular book *With Kitchener to Khartoum* published the same year by the enterprising journalist G W Steevens. The racy immediacy of the account was a revelation to those at home and whetted the appetites of adventurous travellers.

Then there had been the Fashoda Incident when Britain and France very nearly came to blows. While Kitchener and the British army had been fighting the Mahdists, in the north of Sudan, the French had come up behind their backs and laid claim to the valley of the upper Nile in Southern Sudan. Captain Jean Baptiste Marchand (1865-1934) had led a French expedition across from West Africa and had established a French post at Fashoda (now Kodok). The French flag had been run up with the intention of extending the area of French influence stretching across from West Africa and the Congo basin.

At the same time, a new Ethiopian Empire had just been created by Menelik II. In 1897 the Russian cavalryman Alexander Bulatovich[29] had gone with Menelik's warlord Ras Giorgis, when he annexed the area lying between the Ethiopian highlands and Lake Rudolf (now Turkana) on behalf of the emperor. As Bulatovich explained, it was 'terra incognita' – no one had yet explored the region northwest of the lake – it was up for grabs. Equatoria, the province formerly held by Emin Pasha for the Egyptians, had been abandoned.

Suddenly this remote corner of Africa hit the headlines and fuelled public imagination and indignation. The old Egyptian post at Fashoda

29 Richard Seltzer, *Ethiopia through Russian Eyes; Country in Transition 1896-1898* (2000). This is the translation from Russian of the two books by Alexander Bulatovich: *From Enttoto to the river Baro* and *With The Armies of Menelik II.*

was a miserable place, hot and malarial. The Egyptians had used it as a kind of Devil's Island for prisoners, but it was now a subject of fascination, key to an explosive situation.

Marchand's 3,000-mile march across Africa had been a tour de force; he had shown extreme bravery making his way past fantastic obstacles to reach the Nile and Southern Sudan. His object was to seize the valley of the Upper Nile in the name of France to join hands with the Emperor Menelik II in Ethiopia and come to an agreement with the Mahdist leader, Khalifa, who was still at large, and above all to forestall the British expedition led by Kitchener that was advancing up the river.

France threatened to back Marchand's stance, almost to the point of war. Kitchener was instructed to treat the situation with kid gloves but the French were to be dislodged at all costs. Kitchener arrived with his flotilla of gunboats outside Fashoda, tactfully wearing a fez and flying the Egyptian flag. He made it clear that he had instructions to take possession of the Upper Nile on behalf of Egypt, its rightful owner. Marchand could not dispute this and Kitchener magnanimously offered to leave Marchand undisturbed until he had communicated with the French government. In the meantime Colonel Jackson, who was given the title of Military and Civil Commandant of the Fashoda District, landed with a contingent of men who raised the Egyptian flag and immediately set up camp alongside the French.

In Britain tempers boiled over. The British thought the French had attempted to rob them of their victory by an underhand trick, while to the French it seemed that this was one more instance of British territorial greed and bullying. The British had abandoned the Sudan after the fall of Khartoum in 1885 and Marchand, by his courageous march, had taken possession. Clearly the Upper Nile now belonged to France.

But in the end the French gave way, as the situation was untenable. It became clear that support from the Ethiopians was not to be relied upon and French military muscle was weak. In December 1898 the French reluctantly lowered their flag over Fashoda and a bitterly disappointed Marchand returned to France. He went via the Sobat River, through

Ethiopia, as he refused to return through British-held Sudan. His personal heroism was hugely admired and the incident struck a chord with the public as one of exceptional daring and audacity.

Nevertheless, on March 21, 1899, the French reluctantly signed an agreement, by which the whole of the Nile Valley was reserved to the British. Seven months later, in October 1899, the Khalifa, the Mahdi's successor, was killed in an attack led by Colonel Reginald Wingate. This signalled, for the time being, the end of the anti-Egyptian movement in Sudan.

Lord Kitchener, who had been made Governor of Khartoum in 1898, went to London to appeal for funds to rebuild Khartoum and fund a Gordon College of Education there. Money poured in as the wealthy citizens of Britain responded to Kitchener's call when he stated bluntly 'those who have conquered are now called upon to civilise.'[30]

In January 1899 the British and Egyptian governments had signed an agreement, which established an Anglo-Egyptian condominium over the Sudan – a hybrid arrangement giving Britain a virtual trusteeship based on right of conquest, which proved extraordinarily successful although without precedent in international law. It lasted until 1956. The watershed between the Nile and Congo Rivers was declared to be the boundary between French and British spheres of Influence.

Thus it was that by 1900 the entire length of the Nile River from Alexandria to Lake Victoria in Uganda lay within the sphere of British influence and was open and safe for travel as it never had been before. There were fortified posts along its length under British military command all the way to the border with Ethiopia and up to Uganda.

In May 1902 further control of the area was achieved when a treaty was signed between Menelik II and the British fixing Ethiopia's western borders and giving the British favourable trading concessions.

---

30 Philip Magnus, *Kitchener: Portrait of an Imperialist* (1958), 146. The new town of Khartoum was laid out in the form of a Union Jack and the Gordon College still survives.

Menelik had then agreed to send his cousin Ras Makonnen, to London, to attend the coronation of Edward VII. Ethiopia, formerly much inclined towards the influence of Russia and France, now realised where the seat of power lay and forged closer diplomatic ties with Britain.

This was the geo-political situation when Northrup decided to organise his first major expedition. It was a uniquely favourable window of opportunity. Menelik II (1844-1913) was at the height of his power. He had expanded his empire south and west, and in the north had defeated the Italians[31] confining them to Eritrea and Somalia. His new capital, Addis Ababa, was fast becoming a wonder of the modern world, as he made use of the latest technology and craftsmen from all parts of the world. In 1897 he had completed a vast reception hall with electric lights where he held huge state banquets. Foreigners were amazed at the spectacle of such power and magnificence. Overseas guests were welcomed and lavishly entertained. Ethiopia was open and accessible for business and tourists from the West. Previously it had

Advance publicity for McMillan's expedition to Ethiopia.

31 Menelik's forces defeated the Italians at the battle of Adua in 1896. The Italians did not recover from the shame of this defeat until 1936, when under Mussolini, they invaded and colonised Ethiopia.

been a country swathed in myth and barbarism, a make believe world, featured in novels by Rider Haggard and John Buchan, tantalising in its mysteriousness. Not any more. British visitors rushed to the capital eager to discuss trade deals, sell goods and go sightseeing.

Ras Makonnen created a good impression in England when he visited in the summer of 1902. He and his entourage dressed in their traditional robes were much feted. He showed himself to be intelligent, pleased to meet new people and was interested in all he saw. He purchased a motorcar, the first imported into Ethiopia.

Accompanying the Ethiopian party was Lieutenant Colonel John Lane Harrington (1865-1927) the British Consul, who knew Ethiopia well as he had lived there since 1897, first as resident agent, then as Consul from 1902.[32] It was he who had persuaded Menelik to allow Ras Mkonnen to visit Britain to attend the coronation and oversaw all the travelling arrangements. He hoped that the visit, and the coronation spectacular, would help secure future British diplomatic and business relations. It was a most successful visit and Harrington went on to have great influence in Ethiopian affairs. He developed a close relationship with the Imperial family.

Northrup, recently returned from his Ethiopian hunting trip, renewed his contact with Ras Mkonnen in London at the earliest opportunity and introduced Lucie to the Ethiopians. He entertained the Ras at his Mayfair home and established such cordial relations that he was given an open invitation to visit Menelik at his court in Addis Ababa. The McMillans also met Harrington, with whom Northrup discussed the idea of leading an expedition to Ethiopia to explore the Blue Nile and Harrington promised his assistance. Harrington became a close family friend and went on to marry Amy McMillan, Northrup's first cousin.[33]

Northrup also had the additional ambition of opening up diplomatic

32 Sir Rennell Rodd had started formal British ties with Ethiopia in 1897, when he led a British Mission to Addis Ababa to meet with Menelik. Harrington was left there as the resident agent.
33 An announcement of their engagement appeared in the *New York Times*, 10 August 1907 and they were married in October that same year. The Harringtons lived in Ethiopia until 1909.

Sir John Harrington with Ras Mkonnen on his visit to England in 1902 to attend the coronation of Edward VII. Front row left to right: Sir John Harrington, Ras Mkonnen and Colonel Bernard Ramsden James (1864-1938), intelligence officer, later military attaché to Washington. Back row left to right: General Fitawari Abba Tabor, unidentified, Chief Priest of Harar, General Fitawari Haile Selassie Abaynah, and Kontiba Gabra Desta (1855-1950) Mayor of Gondar and the emperor's special envoy to the Khalifa at Omdurman.

relations between America and Ethiopia. As yet America had no representative in Ethiopia despite having a brisk trade in *merikani* (American cotton) and coffee. (It was not until December 1903 that Robert Skinner, the US Consul General in Marseilles, led an American Mission to Ethiopia, endorsed by President Theodore Roosevelt to formalise trading agreements.)

With plenty of money and time on his hands Northrup felt this was an opportunity too good to miss. A chance for everything he had ever dreamed of – all rolled into one. Exploration, hunting and new business all conveniently located in Africa at high altitude.

In the scrapbooks kept by Lucie McMillan, there are a large number of newspaper cuttings reporting on the preparations for this Blue Nile expedition[34]. There was considerable publicity surrounding

34 *The Globe, The Graphic, The Morning Post* and the *St Louis Post-Dispatch* all carried stories about the Blue Nile exploration party led by the American millionaire from St Louis.

the adventurous undertaking, which was reported in the British and French press as well as the local papers of St Louis. French journalists were concerned as they suspected the British were trying to divert Ethiopian trade away from the French port of Jibuti, while the British press played on their fears. From the newspaper reports we learn that on his arrival in Addis Ababa Northrup intended to seek an audience with the Emperor and introduce himself as a wealthy American capitalist looking for commercial opportunities in Ethiopia. He was going to ask the Emperor for a gold mining concession, and while he was at it, permission to explore the Blue Nile and hunt.

The Blue Nile was full of cataracts and dangerous rapids, but Northrup was undaunted. He planned to see if the river could be navigated with modern boats and new technology and used as an alternative and quicker route between Ethiopia and Egypt. Brash and foolhardy, he was eager for adventure and exploration, the ultimate dream of an adrenaline junkie of the early 20th century.

In that era adventure trips on the grand scale always had to be taken with a 'Purpose' in mind and preferably go somewhere that had not been

A map of Ethiopia and Sudan showing the Nile River and the area where Northrup travelled on his explorations.

explored before. It was not enough to travel simply for personal amusement. On return it was expected that the trip be written up in a suitably erudite manner, the book beautifully bound in tooled leather, and the brave adventurers then be elected fellows of the Royal

Geographical Society, the headquarters for world exploration. This was the ultimate accolade, which gave the required kudos to the expedition and made all the expense and discomfort worthwhile. The daring and resourceful explorer could then sink back and enjoy the admiration of the populace for decades to come and endlessly bore his friends and relations with tales of his exploits.

Northrup began the preparations for his expedition in the autumn of 1902. No expense was spared. Four especially designed steel boats, in sections, were sent on ahead to Addis Ababa with vast amounts of equipment. He hired Burchart Heinrich Jessen, a Norwegian engineer and surveyor, who was given the task of assembling and taking a steam launch, called the *Addis Abeba*, up the Blue Nile from Khartoum. The idea was that the McMillan party in the steel punts would proceed downstream, riding the rapids, from the north, where they would meet up with Jessen coming from the other direction.

In February 1903 Northrup gathered his men and equipment at Jibuti and travelled by train to Dire Dawa and then by mule to Harar and on to Addis Ababa. On this trip Northrup was accompanied by William Marlow his valet, Mr Morgan-Browne, his secretary and right hand man, an American friend Isidore Morse, and a Colonel Fairfax, who joined the party at the last minute. Their progress was slow as this was both a hunting trip as well as a scientific expedition.

In Harar the governor, Ras Makonnen welcomed his old friend, Northrup, most heartily and placed his palace at the disposal of the visitors. They stayed for several days and were royally entertained. At Harar they picked up a Monsieur Dubois Desaulle, a journalist on the *Figaro* newspaper, who was on his way to Addis Ababa. Desaulle unfortunately wandered off one day from the main group and was murdered. His death was avenged when the murderer – from the Dinka tribe – was apprehended, taken back to Harar, convicted and then hung. This caused further delay and Northrup did not reach Addis Ababa until May 1903.

The arrival of an American millionaire in Addis Ababa created quite a stir and another flurry of newspaper articles. Northrup met the emperor and presented him with a Colt rapid-fire revolver, personally demonstrating to him how it worked. Menelik appreciated the present and liked the jovial, large young American and invited him to a state banquet.

Menelik II was an absolute monarch ruling over a medieval feudal country; nothing was done in Ethiopia without the emperor's approval and signed letters of permission. All visiting foreigners wishing to hunt or explore or engage in commercial activity had to present themselves at court with their sponsor. Harrington promoted Northrup most successfully; he and the emperor became friends during his stay.

An idea of what conditions were like in Addis Ababa when Northrup visited can be read in Major Percy Powell Cotton's account of his hunting trip to Ethiopia in 1900.[35] Here Powell Cotton attended a state banquet. Suitably attired in evening dress, Powell Cotton went with Harrington, who was in full military uniform, to the palace enclosure. This was a half hour ride away from the British Agency Compound, where he was staying and where Northup also stayed in 1903. Here is what Powell Cotton recorded:

> After a weary wait of nearly an hour, we were ushered into the great hall or Aderash and conducted to a dais, the centre of which was taken up by a very handsome throne, covered by a canopy 18ft square, made of velvet with an M in gold surmounted by an imperial crown and supported by pillars of gold picked out in red and green, the present of the French Government to Menelik. The Emperor was half-reclining on a settee in front of the throne, supported by pink silk cushions and surrounded by court officials and attendants, who ministered to his wants from a white-clothed table bearing an enormous pile of the thin cakes of native bread called injerra...

35 PHG Powell Cotton FZS FRGS, *A Sporting Trip through Abyssinia* (1902). Major Powell Cotton (1866-1940) was a wealthy Englishman, who travelled extensively and though interested in hunting initially was later primarily a naturalist and anthropologist. He left a complete account of his travels in his meticulous diaries, which can be seen at the Powell Cotton Museum he set up at Quex Park, Birchington. Although he travelled the same routes as Northrup, sometimes only a few months apart, they never met.

The dais was curtained off from the rest of the hall by thin, flowery-patterned chintz curtains. Passing behind the throne, we took our seats at two tables laid on the Emperor's left – the eleven diplomats at one, and we four travellers at the other. The Rases and chief generals were divided into two groups, to the right and left of the Emperor. Our tables were laid in European fashion, with massive silver-handled knives and forks bearing the royal cypher. The service was of Sevres Porcelain emblazoned with the Lion of Judah. (Then follows the elaborate menu they were served – ten courses plus all the different wines).

While we were being served a continuous stream of dishes were carried in for the Emperor's table by female slaves. (Then follows a description of the ceremony of tasting for poison). Many of the dishes he just touched and sent on to the chief officers sitting round him, which is considered a great honour. One a sort of rich stew covered with chilli sauce, he sent out to our tables, but it was a dish to be approached with caution by any but an Anglo-Indian. Beside each group of officers stood an attendant, holding shoulder-high a great piece of raw beef killed that morning, from which, with a small sharp knife, each officer cut thin slices and placing a small portion in his mouth cut off the remainder close to his lips. Each had his decanter of tej, covered with a piece of silk, from which he took long draughts. When the Emperor drank those round held up their garments to screen him from all chance of the evil eye...

When lunch was over the curtains were drawn back disclosing to view the fine hall. The walls are covered with blue paper and gold stars and the roof timbers painted white are picked out in the national colours. The attendants were busy setting out round baskets piled with flat cakes of bread in rows on the floor. The great double doors at the end of the hall were then thrown open and the hall soon began to fill with guests, who as they advanced towards the Emperor with their right shoulder bared, bowed low and took their places in little groups of ten or a dozen round each basket. The centre aisle nearest the dais was reserved for priests, while the officers sat on either side of them. The soldiers filled the remainder of the hall until over 4,000 guests were being regaled.

A steward holding a great piece of raw beef and a handful of small sharp knives placed himself by each group of priests and officers, while to save time the soldiers were served with portions already cut. To each was handed a horn cup, nearly a foot long, filled with tej. Meanwhile, an Abyssinian brass band played a selection of music, including the national airs of France, Russia and England. (The band had been trained by a Russian musician in 1897). As the first detachment of guests finished their bread and meat they were each given a small glass of araki and ushered out by great doors at the end of the aisles, on either side of the dais.

The breadbaskets and tej horns were then replenished and another 4,000 hungry guests were admitted. After this the Europeans left as they had already spent three hours at the feast, but another group of guests was already waiting their turn outside.[36]

Powell Cotton also gave a detailed description of Menelik as he appeared at state audiences:

> The Emperor was installed in a small state chair with a carpet spread at his feet. He was dressed in white trousers, brown, clocked socks, very large patent leather dress shoes with no laces, a long coat of green silk with yellow stripes and a black satin burnous embroidered with gold down the front and the hood lined with pink silk. In the left ear he wore a rose-cut diamond stud. His head was bound with a piece of white muslin, drawn tightly across the scalp with the edges rolled and tied behind. On the top of this was placed a large-crowned, broad

---

36 ibid, 127-9.

brimmed straw hat, covered with gold leaf, the band dotted round with rubies and sapphires. On the little finger of his left hand gleamed a diamond ring and another set with a miniature watch. Over the emperor was held a red silk umbrella, heavily embroidered and fringed with gold.[37]

In his diaries Powell Cotton described the Emperor as a small man, having a dark pockmarked complexion, good-humoured with a hearty laugh.

Major Powell Cotton in hunting attire.

Northrup made such a marked impression on the Emperor that Menelik awarded his large visitor two medals as a sign of his favour, of which Northrup was immensely proud. He received the Star of Ethiopia, usually given to visiting dignitaries, and was also made a member of the Order of the Cross of Solomon.[38] During Menelik's reign medals were given out somewhat haphazardly and with great frequency and were often embellished with real jewels and precious stones. Designed by Russian or French goldsmiths, the medals and crosses were hung on lavishly decorated collars or ribbons in western style. It was John Harrington who later reorganised the categories of Ethiopian medals and introduced a system of ranking similar to that of British honours.

At long last all arrangements for the eagerly awaited and much publicised expedition were complete. A large number of porters had been employed, the luxurious stores had been gathered and the steel

37 ibid, 122.
38 The order of Solomon was later only awarded to monarchs and heads of state.

Flat bottomed steel boats similar to these were carried in sections by mule from Addis Ababa to Kutia where they were assembled, an operation which took six days.

boats had arrived.[39] In June 1903, (a strange time to begin as it was the start of the rainy season, but perhaps chosen because they hoped the river waters would be at their calmest if not at their lowest level) the explorers set off from Addis Ababa.

There was Northrup McMillan, his personal servant William Marlow,[40] Mr Morgan Browne, his aide, a hunting friend, Mr Isidore Morse of Boston,[41] Mr Lang a mining engineer, Dr Koreander of the Russian Medical Mission and Mr Clark of the British Legation.[42] A

39 Article, *Daily Mail*, 29 January 1903. These boats were made of galvanised sheet steel and were built in nine floatable sections. They were 19 feet in length, had a 4 feet 6inches beam and each carried six men and 500 pounds of baggage.
40 The 1901 UK census lists William Marlow aged 23 as a footman in the McMillan London establishment. Stephen J North in his list of Europeans in British East Africa prior to 1906 records him as a settler living at Juja Farm in 1905, when he applies for a landholder's game licence.
41 It is not absolutely clear whether Isidore Morse did or did not join this part of the expedition, though it was originally intended that he would. With only four boats space was limited to 24 persons; four steersmen and 20 paddlers.
42 Burchart Heinrich Jessen, *W N McMillan's Expeditions and Big-game Hunting in Sudan, Abyssinia and British East Africa* (1906), 4.

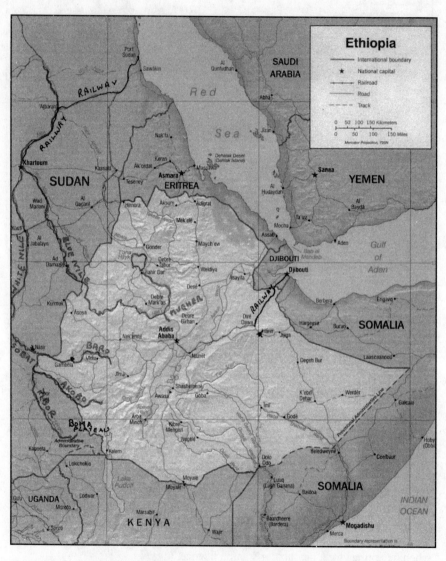

*A map of Ethiopia showing the rivers and areas explored
by Northrup McMillan during the years 1902-1905.*

caravan of a hundred camels carried all the stores and equipment. They started off with much fanfare.

The four flat-bottomed steel boats were carried in sections by mule from Addis Ababa down to the confluence of the Mugher and the Abbai (Blue Nile), at a place called Kutia. Here the boats were assembled, a difficult operation which took six days as the joints would not fit.[43]

The Mugher, a tributary of the Blue Nile, rises near Addis Ababa and flows into the main river at a point not far from the town of Debre Markos. (Nowadays it is the site of a cement factory and a modern bridge.) Northrup's start off point therefore was about 100 miles from Bahar Dar, where the Blue Nile rises in Lake Tana, well beyond the insurmountable obstacle of the Tis Abay (Tissisat) Falls and past the first large loop of the river.

Taking the shortest and most direct route from the capital, Addis Ababa, as the crow flies, through to the Sudan, made logical sense on a map if not on the ground. No doubt Northrup hoped to bypass the worst of the turbulence and at the point where he started the Blue Nile seemed wider and calmer. But appearances were deceptive. Further on the river suddenly narrowed and dipped into a steep gorge where the waters rushed over jagged boulders on a headlong course down towards the plains. Even at low water the current was deadly and the people who lived near its banks viewed the river with well-founded dread.

For the first few miles everything went well but then a difficult cataract was encountered. One boat was upset and the other sank and broke up, thus depriving the expedition of their stores and most of the ammunition, making it impossible to proceed further. Very short of food, they walked back to the capital. The flat-bottomed steel boats, built with buoyancy compartments so they would float, had fallen to pieces at the first challenge of the river. Northrup had thought the steel boats strong and unsinkable.

Meanwhile Jessen in the launch *Addis Abeba* was steaming towards the frontier. He made the low water ascent of the cataracts at Roseires

---

43 ibid, 4.

Baluchi ivory traders about 1900.

and Famakka, but turned back before reaching the Ethiopian border, when he heard the news of the failure at the other end.

The expedition had been a total disaster; the steel boats had fallen apart within a few hours at the first contact with the rapids. Nothing had been achieved. Nevertheless, the McMillan expedition is recorded in all accounts of European exploration of the Blue Nile, as it was the first serious attempt undertaken since 1821, when the Frenchman, Frederic Cailliaud, had attempted to sail up the Blue Nile in search of gold and slaves. Cailliaud had reached the Ethiopian border, but had stopped at Fazugli where the Blue Nile had vanished into an enormous gorge, impassable even to men on foot.

On his return to England, Northrup gave a short interview to the Times, explaining the fate of his expedition. This is what he had to say:

At 8 in the morning our flotilla of four steel punts, each having one steersman and five paddlers, commenced the journey. For seven hours our heavily laden craft encountered one set of rapids after another. The river varied from 60 yards to 150 yards in width and ran through a deep ravine with mountainous banks. In many places the water was alive with crocodiles and hippos. At 4 o'clock in the afternoon we came to the set of rapids where we were wrecked. We encamped on the rocky banks in a sorry plight, for our food consisted of one tin of biscuits and some preserved ginger. We succeeded in putting up our tents but that night a hurricane sprang up and our tent was in continual danger of being carried away. We spent a miserable time, but at last got to sleep, only to be roused at 4 in the morning by the wild screams of one of our people, a Somali, who had been seized by a big crocodile, which had crawled up the rocks. The brute had seized his victim by the head and dragged him to the water's edge. By throwing stones at the crocodile we succeeded in making him leave the Somali, who, although terribly mauled, eventually recovered. After remaining for two days we started on the way back to the capital, and had not gone far before small pox broke out in the caravan. After seven days' march we arrived at Addis Ababa where we spent a week. I again saw the Emperor and obtained his permission to once more attempt to navigate the Blue Nile. He promised every assistance, but again advised me to abandon the idea. We now marched back to the head of the railway…[44]

Far away while hunting in the Lado Enclave Major Powell Cotton noted down in his diary some amusing tales he had been told.

One of these involved a couple of white men who were trying to cross the Nile in an American steel boat. A monster crocodile, who lived in the depths of the river, was disturbed and had come up from the deep and pierced several holes in the airtight compartments of their boat so that such a quantity of water rushed in that they sank and only just escaped with their lives![45]

44 "American Exploration in Abyssinia," *The Times*, 12 October 1903.
45 Powell Cotton, Diary transcripts, February 1905.

CHAPTER IV

THE SECOND EXPEDITION:
ALONG THE NILE AND INTO THE SUDAN
AND ETHIOPIA

O n his return to London in autumn 1903, Northrup decided to organise another expedition to Sudan and Ethiopia to coincide with the English winter months. This time Lucie insisted on coming too. Northrup now planned to try out the Sobat River route.[46] The French explorer, Marchand, had already successfully navigated the Sobat River, but there was still the maze of smaller tributaries and marshy areas along the southwestern borders of Ethiopia, which had not been completely mapped and explored. The stated object of the expedition was 'to survey the unknown countries between Lake Baro and Lake Rudolf (now Lake Turkana) and to do some hunting and collecting of animal, bird and butterfly specimens for British Museums.' The whole thing was to be done more professionally than the Blue Nile debacle, with some serious experts joining the venture.

This expedition is well documented and we get a clear idea of what

---

46 The Sobat River is a tributary of the Nile, which flows from Lake Baro in Ethiopia, and joins the Nile in Southern Sudan at a point further to the south than the Blue Nile, just beyond the present town of Malakal.

happened virtually day by day. Not only did Jessen continue with his account of McMillan's travels, but Charles Bulpett, the expedition manager, also published a book,[47] and Lucie McMillan kept a journal. Jessen, who was not writing in his native tongue, tends to be rather difficult to follow, while Bulpett, a former barrister, had a good command of the English language and is much easier to read. Bulpett used many quotes from Lucie's journal, which was written in a lively and amusing style, and it is evident that they enjoyed each other's company and sense of humour. [48]

On the expedition came:

Northrup McMillan, who footed the bill and was accompanied by his personal servant William Marlow, who had been with him on the Blue Nile Expedition.

Lucie McMillan with her maid Louise Decker. Louise Decker (1850-1938) sometimes described as the daughter of a black American slave, was in fact more probably of German extraction. She had looked after Lucie since birth. She is listed in 1870 in a US census when Lucie aged three years, had just lost her mother, and was living in Vermont. She is also listed in the 1901 British census as a ladies maid, when

---

47 C W Bulpett, *A Picnic Party in Wildest Africa; Being a Sketch of a Winter's Trip to some of the Unknown Waters of the Upper Nile* (1907). It was printed for private distribution and very few original copies were made. The copy I saw in the Royal Geographical Society (RGS) had never been taken off the shelf. In recent years, however, it has been reprinted and can be read on the internet.

48 The opening paragraph of Bulpett's book gives an idea of the man and his whimsical style. He introduces his book with these words: "There are picnics and there are picnics! Some people prefer to take their outings on the bank of the Thames or in the sylvan retreats of rural England. I suppose it was a desire for novelty and perhaps also a little spirit of adventure that led us to do our picnicking in less frequented regions. Grouse shooting in Scotland is good, deer stalking in the Highlands is uncommonly fine sport, but grouse shooting and deer stalking must fall short in interest and excitement to sport and exploration in an unknown land." He then goes on to explain how it was Mr McMillan an American gentleman resident in England, who with a "praiseworthy desire to combine pleasure with utility" had suggested to him the idea of this expedition. He praises "the sense of freedom and unrestraint; the mental exhilaration that traversing an unknown and unexplored country gives."

the McMillans were living in London. She remained with her mistress until her death in 1938 and is buried on Ol Donyo Sabuk. Lucie, who was very fond of Louise, founded the Louise Decker Home, for elderly Europeans of small means, in her memory.

Sir John Harrington was in charge of the Sobat Expedition. Lt Col Sir JL Harrington had been knighted in the New Year's Honours List of 1903 and been appointed 'British Minister Plenipotentiary in Abyssinia.' He was now on his way back to Addis Ababa and joined the group with his personal servant, Towell. This it seems was a godsend as his foresight and personal influence enabled the party to receive special treatment and assistance.[49]

Charles W L Bulpett, general manager and overseer of the Boma expedition.

John Destro and the Willsden tent.

Charles Bulpett, who became a permanent fixture in the McMillan household as a result of this adventure, was a keen sportsman and avid hunter. He had already been on a hunting expedition in the Upper Nile valley four years previously and therefore knew the area. He was the oldest member of the party. Charles William Lloyd Bulpett was born August 18th 1859 at Sandgates, Chertsey. He was a sportsman and athlete, educated at Rugby and Oxford. As a young man he played cricket at Lords for Middlesex and was a useful batsman and fast bowler. Later he trained as a barrister, and was called to the bar in 1888 at Lincolns Inn Fields. However, his legal career was not successful enough to support his preferred life style as a sporting gentleman about town. His lack of funds led him to become

49 Bulpett gave credit especially to Sir John Harrington, "who on his way to a diplomatic post kindly put his expertise and authority at our disposal and to his help and forethought the expedition owed much of its success."

a professional hanger on, and a fix-it man, who became indispensable to the McMillans. He stayed on with Lucie after her husband's death and died in 1939 at Chiromo, Nairobi. A confirmed bachelor, he liked to hint at disappointment in love. According to Edward Paice, he was famous for swimming the Thames at Greenwich in a frock coat and top hat for a wager and claimed to have been ruined by a courtesan of legendary beauty and lack of scruples.[50]

Dr Charles Singer (1876-1960), a trained zoologist and medical doctor, who provided much amusement on the trip, but proved worth his salt, learning to be an excellent shot and naturalist, while keeping everyone in good health. He was interested in insects and small mammals.[51]

Philip Photius Constantine Zaphiro (1879 –1933) a Greek born in Constantinople, who was employed by Harrington as a taxidermist and interpreter. He had lived in Harar, Ethiopia, where he worked as a medical dispenser for some years and spoke Arabic, Amharic and Oromo (Galla as it was then called). He was also a keen ornithologist. In 1907 he was appointed British Southern Abyssinia Frontier Inspector.[52] He became First Interpreter at the Legation under the Minister Wilfrid Thesiger (1909-1920) and in 1921 was appointed Oriental Secretary and was given a royal commission.[53]

John Destro, Northrup's aide and secretary. John Destro (1882 –1952) was born in Venice. He immigrated to England in 1901 and met the McMillans in London, where he was employed by Northrup. He stayed on with the McMillans and eventually became farm manager at

---

50 Edward Paice, *Lost Lion of Empire* (2001),199.

51 He named an Ethiopian rat after Sir John Harrington in appreciation for his help. Harrington's Rat (*Desmomys Harringtoni*) is a rare species of rodent found only in Ethiopia.

52 His job was to prevent Somalis taking over wells that belonged to other tribes (notably the Boran) and to make sure the Abyssinians and Somalis stayed on their side of the border, a very difficult task. "Zaphiro somehow or other had acquired an Admiral's frock coat and red cummerbund in which he rode about the frontier persuading the tribesmen to do as he told them – apparently quite often they did." Elspeth Huxley, *Out in the Midday Sun (1985)*, 151.

53 Cynthia Salvadori, *Slaves and Ivory Continued*, (2010), 432.

Donyo Sabuk. In 1913 he married Clara Sehof, and in 1915 he left the employ of the McMillans to start his own dairy business at Burnbrae, Nairobi, called the Villa Franca Dairy. He was a great friend of Louise Decker.[54]

Burchart Heinrich Jessen, born in 1866, a Norwegian, engineer and cartographer, in charge of the boats, who we have already met.

Counting the boats' crews and the Somali and Abyssinian servants, the expedition started off with a grand total of 43 persons. Later on the number of porters employed fluctuated, rising at certain times to almost 400.

Waiting on the quayside at Khartoum was an immense mountain of equipment, tents, foodstuffs and other stores. Jessen was appalled when he saw how much there was as he could not imagine how it could all be transported.

As the expedition manager Bulpett devotes a long chapter in his book headed 'Our Equipment.'[55] He goes on at length about the importance of the right type of tent and how the various makes and types compare. Bulpett himself favoured an Indian type made at Cawnpore and said it should be made of Willsden canvas and measure ten feet by ten feet with an outer fly and groundsheet with a bathroom area at the back. The whole tent weighed an astonishing 250 pounds and took four porters to carry. He went on to recommend tinned foods, and oatmeal, dried milk, sugar, salt and flour all stored in airtight tins. In his opinion the right kind of equipment and foodstuffs were vital and the lack thereof was the reason many expeditions had failed in the past. A Berthon collapsible boat was also deemed essential. Bulpett went on to list the personnel needed for the smooth operation of an expedition and laid particular emphasis on employing a good headman, the lynchpin, because he was the buffer between the white leaders and their porters. Bulpett recommended for this position a man from Aden

---

54 Trzebinski archives, Bodleian Library, Box 1. John Destro had four children, who all remained in Kenya. Clara Sehof his wife was originally from South Africa. Her family came to farm in Kenya in 1906. In 1939 Destro moved to Embakasi. He also owned a coffee farm at Kiambu.
55 Bulpett, 4-14.

or Berbera. And of course there had to be tent boys, cooks, shikaris (gun bearers) and last but not least scores of porters and mules. The whole operation sounded very much like equipping an army on the move and the manager, the general, in over-all command.

For transportation there was the steam launch, *Addis Abeba*; this was the same boat from the previous expedition and was waiting for them at Khartoum[56]. It was forty foot long, had a draft of 24 inches, when loaded and had a maximum speed of 6 knots. For himself and the chief members of the expedition, Northrup had ordered a luxurious new steam launch, appropriately named the Sobat. At 75 feet long with a maximum speed of just over 9 knots it was the largest and fastest of the McMillan 'fleet'. It was able to sleep nine people and was comfortably appointed, with an upper viewing deck.[57] The Vosper engines, most importantly, could run either on wood or oil and it was almost flat bottomed, having a draft of just over 20 inches. There was also an eighteen foot oil motor launch referred to as 'the Naptha launch' and two rowing boats, one of tin and one of canvas. All of these had been ordered in sections and were assembled on arrival, under the watchful eye of Jessen, the engineer. In addition there were two big barges,[58] or punts, built at Khartoum, for carrying the stores and the men. It was a veritable flotilla and too cumbersome to move on its own. In the end the Government Steamer was hired to pull the whole lot up to Nasser (Nasir), a point on the Sobat River some miles past the confluence with the White Nile. There is a photograph in Jessen's account showing how the various McMillan crafts were lashed to the sides of the big government paddle steamer.

---

56 It had been built at Brimscombe, near Stroud, and had been transhipped to Alexandria in 1903, lashed to the forward port deck on the Moss line steamer, Nitocris and then taken by train to Khartoum. It had suffered considerable damage en route and Northrup had learnt by his mistakes and the new boats for this expedition were all ordered in sections and were far easier to transport.

57 Jessen, 45. The boat was fitted up with two cabins, the forward had accommodation for three persons and the after one for six.

58 Also referred to as punts by Jessen. These were forty feet by ten feet and carried the stores and wood fuel, as well as the men and some livestock. They also carried three tons of fuel oil.

While last minute preparations were going on, Lucie looked round Khartoum. She disdainfully reported that "Khartoum is an uninteresting town, save for the association of Gordon and the Mahdi." The climate was very hot and she complained of the strong wind which "blows dust and sand into ones eyes and is generally demoralising to the feminine hair and the toilet' but she thought the nights beautiful beyond words."[59]

On the morning of the 25th January 1904 they started up the White Nile. To begin with they steamed leisurely up the river, and life on board was very pleasant - not unlike a boating trip on the Mississippi! Northrup did some duck shooting and fishing, while Lucie supervised the cooking which was of gourmet standard. Even then in his early 30's Northrup was a large man. Jessen described him as six foot three inches tall and weighing over 20 stone. He commented that he was a big eater and wrote that he would consume two shoulders of mutton with vegetables, at a sitting. His intake of alcohol was

The Fort at Fashoda.

also considerable, as he would drink a bottle of champagne and most of a bottle of brandy a day.[60]

The European members of the expedition got to know one another well. For entertainment there was a gramophone and games of bridge and whist and there was plenty of sporting talk amongst the men. As one of the amusements on board, Lucie decided to give her fellow travellers nicknames[61] and made it a fineable offence to address anyone by his or her proper name. Lucie was known as 'The Nuisance' as

59 Bulpett,16.
60 Randall Swift, Bodleian Library, Rhodes House, Mss Afr.s.2154 –12/1. Later on in the year Swift travelled on the same ship as Northrup.
61 Bulpett, 19.

Sir John Harrington disapproved of women coming on expeditions, insisting they would be nothing but a nuisance. But Jessen was full of praise for Lucie and thought she showed great fortitude and courage throughout, while her maid Miss Louise's performance was "simply marvellous." Bulpett agreed with Jessen, that Lucie was anything but a nuisance. Sir John was called 'The Chief' because of his commanding manner, while Charles Bulpett was christened 'Uncle' because he was a confirmed old bachelor, or by Lucie, who had a soft spot for him, 'Don Carlos.' Northrup was called 'Merodi Sahib' or the elephant man by the Somalis, because of his great size and appetite, while Dr Singer, was known as 'the Baby,' although he was not the youngest on the expedition.

The temperature started to rise as the mimosa bushes on the outskirts of Khartoum gave way to reeds and elephant grass along the banks. The scenery became increasingly monotonous, broken only by the occasional native village. The mosquitoes were ferocious and plentiful and they encountered a lot more insects, including the Zerut fly – "an insect about an inch long, which had a nasty bite, leaving a lump as big as an egg, but was not fatal to humans," fortunately! The thermometer reached 107 Fahrenheit as they steamed towards Kodok, formerly Fashoda.[62]

As they progressed up-river further into Southern Sudan, the people began to change becoming darker and less Arab of feature. First there were the Shilluk, great cattle breeders, who lived near Kodok, and were instantly recognisable by their white clay hairstyles done up in fantastic shapes. At Kodok they paid a courtesy call on the British governor, Colonel Matthews, who was in charge of the small fortification, which since 1900 had come under Anglo-Egyptian rule.

Then further up-river, they entered Nuer territory. Lucie described them as a large and dark people, mostly naked with a habit of knocking out their lower teeth and styling their hair with red cow dung. Lucie found them quite frightening at first sight, but admired their dexterous

---

62 It was here in 1898 that the infamous stand off between Kitchener and the French explorer Marchand took place.

The Sobat towing the smaller boats up the Nile.

technique of spearing a fish with a single thrust of a lance. There were mosquitoes in profusion and plenty of fish.

A couple of days up from Kodok, the expedition stopped at an American mission station on the banks. They visited the missionaries and asked about their work and learned that they were working hard to convert the Nuers and Shilluk to Christianity[63]

On reaching Fort Nasser, 1,000 miles up-stream from Khartoum, where there was a small fort under the command of Captain Headlam, the government paddle steamer could go no further, as the river levels had become too low for it to continue.[64] The flotilla was dismantled and the expedition boats continued on under their own steam. They made very slow progress as their main launch the Sobat towed the smaller boats. Bulpett described how the river became so shallow in places that "several times we had our devoted crew of Sudanese jump into the water, to tread out a passage through the soft sand, while we stood at the bows and constantly fired our rifles to frighten away the

---

63 This according to Cynthia Salvadori is probably the mission station at Obel.
64 Bulpett had sad memories of Nasser (modern day spelling Nasir) as it was here, on his expedition four years previously, that his companion had died as a result of a hunting accident. Lucie became sick (possibly malaria), but recovered after a few days.

crocodiles."[65] They began to run out of oil and had to cut down wood to provide fuel for the boilers. Whenever suitable trees were spotted everyone had to go on woodcutting duties, which was hard work in the extreme heat.

The members of the expedition did a considerable amount of hunting throughout the trip, less for sport than to provide meat for themselves, the porters and the crews. The McMillans had brought along seven hunting dogs, a cross between lurcher and whippet, but they proved totally unsuited to the terrain and ended up being used as pets and guard dogs. Lucie, who was very fond of animals, became most distressed when two of her dogs were injured in a fight and were put down. Northrup shot a great number of hippos, which were in profusion in the river, although the Muslim Somalis and Sudanese would not eat the hippo meat as they saw it as a form of pork, a proscribed meat.

Further along trees became increasingly scarce, and the banks covered in elephant grass became too steep to climb out easily. Supplies of wood and provisions became dangerously low. They decided to stop and sent Jessen back to Nasir for wood and stores, so they could continue. Bulpett described how Jessen worked very hard, keeping the boats running and fetching the fuel and provisions and how his stoic determination under difficult conditions was invaluable.

While Jessen went back to Nasir, the rest of the party made temporary camp. Lucie named it 'Camp Desolation.' They were camped on a dry black plain and were troubled with dust storms and had to eat crocodile eggs. Fights broke out amongst the men and Northrup fell ill. For a short while he was unable to eat, his wife became seriously concerned, but he recovered after a few days and his usual hearty appetite returned.

Jessen returned towing the barges filled with wood, sooner than expected. This was a great relief to all and the expedition continued.

On February 20th they arrived at the mouth of a tributary called Adura and camped on the opposite bank of the river close to a Nuer

65 Bulpett, 31.

*Lucie McMillan posing as Diana the huntress on the
banks of the Nile holding a spear with one of her dogs.*

village called Kaig, 120 miles from Nasir. The Sobat had now become
the Baro, (the name changes at the point where the Pibor River joins
the Sobat). They set up a permanent camp at Kaig, which was a
pleasant scenic spot with an abundance of wild animals and Jessen
was sent back again to collect stores and equipment from Nasir. Lucie
christened this camp: 'Camp Toolong!' Here they waited until the river
waters rose and Jessen returned, about three weeks in all.

Kaig[66] was situated in the Enclave of Itang.[67] This bit of borderland real estate had been leased by Anglo-Egyptian Sudan from Menelik II in 1902 as a trade depot.[68] When the McMillans arrived at Kaig, they found a number of Greek traders and others who had come up-river from Khartoum and were marooned, and were waiting for the waters to rise. Attracted by the new British trading concession, they were trying to reach Itang, where they intended to start up businesses. They also met a Russian couple on their way to Khartoum travelling in a small sailboat. The Baro, which widens at this point,[69] was seen by both Britain and Ethiopia as an excellent highway for exporting coffee and other produce from the fertile western highlands of Ethiopia to Sudan and Egypt and a free port was later established at Gambela, in 1907.[70]

The surrounding countryside was rich in wildlife[71] and the McMillan party settled down to a leisurely camp routine, enjoying the shooting opportunities, and exploring the river. They had been given hunting permits to shoot as much game as they wanted in Ethiopia, the only restriction being elephant, of which they were allowed only one each. They shot tiang and white-eared cob as well as several giraffe and quantities of antelope.

Life in camp was still fairly luxurious, and Bulpett makes use of a telling quote from Lucie's diary describing how "we are used to having fresh hams sent from Khartoum, which have almost been a cause of divorce between my husband and myself as I think he eats more

66 Kaig nowadays is listed as a populated area latitude 8.18 North and longitude 34.01 East, but I have not been able to locate it on any map. Jessen described it as a small village situated about a mile in from the river.
67 This tiny British territory a few hundred hectares in size was bounded by the Baro to the south, a tributary to the west, a patch of forest to the east and a small conical hill to its north.
68 Itang nowadays is a UN Refugee camp on the Sudanese border, which then became the Sudanese Peoples Liberation Army (SPLA) headquarters and recruitment camp. It is where John Garang lived with his troops.
69 Probably the reason why both Bulpett and Jessen refer to it as Lake Baro.
70 Gambela became a prosperous trade centre as ships from Khartoum sailed in regularly during the rainy season when the water was high, taking seven days down river and 11 days upriver.
71 Now Gambela National Park.

than his share!"[72] Jessen returned fortunately with more hams, so divorce proceedings were averted.

Once Jessen had returned in early March, they laboriously moved camp up-river to an area 10 miles beyond Itang, called Pokum and pitched their tents at Olea, which was a small outlying Yambo village. Bulpett preferred the Yambo[73] to the Nuer, as they were according to him more amenable and willing to work as porters. The chief of Olea village was a woman, and both

Louise Decker riding her mule in Ethiopia.

Itang and Olea were tributaries to the Ethiopian ruler at Gore up in the nearby highlands. As it was the dry season, the villagers were starving, and were very pleased to receive gifts of meat from Northrup's hunting trips in return for providing porters, when needed. Harrington was angered to hear of reports of Ethiopian looting and slaving in these Yambo villages. The Emperor Menelik II had signed an agreement to stop slaving, but obviously little was being done to enforce it.

As Harrington had to get to his new post in Addis Ababa as soon as possible, he had arranged to have mules sent to meet him near the border. A messenger went to collect them from Bure. With the arrival of the mules, the expedition split up. Lucie with her maid Louise, John Destro, and Dr Singer went with Harrington first by boat to Gambela and then rode overland to Addis Ababa via Bure and Gore. Charles Bulpett went with this group as far as Gore, in order to purchase mules

72 Bulpett, 62.

73 The Yambo are now generally referred to as the Anuak.

so that the second stage of the expedition could begin. Northrup, Zaphiro, Marlow and Jessen, stayed behind hunting and enjoying camp life, until Bulpett returned.

There is an amusing section in the Bulpett account about how Lucie's faithful companion Louise had never ridden on a mule and to begin with was horrified at the thought and refused to do so. So they decided to carry her in a kind of home made sedan chair. However, this was most uncomfortable as the porters were not used to the work and when they tried slinging it between two mules it was even worse. So in the end Louise agreed to learn how to ride a mule, and she did it very well.

From the Baro valley there was a steep climb into the Ethiopian highlands, which severely tested the resilience of the travellers. Bulpett wrote that the porters had to be whipped to keep them from running away. At Bure, at the start of the Ethiopian Highlands, Lucie was surprised to see such cultivated and fertile land, quite different from the landscape of Southern Sudan. She also noticed how the Galla people were treated like serfs by their Ethiopian overlords. She met the Governor of the Province, Shaka Tacalin. The travellers experienced the Ethiopian custom, called Durgos, of giving food and presents to passing strangers. Lucie called it a kind of tribute, but noted that the recipient was expected to give rather more in return. She apparently reached Addis Ababa almost destitute due to this system of welcome![74]

Lucie's belief in female equality was dealt a severe blow when she saw how the natives grovelled on the ground whenever Bulpett or Harrington passed, but gave barely a nod for her because she was a woman. "It is no place for an independent American woman!" she remarked.[75] She was also upset by the way the people covered their mouths and faces, as if she was carrying the plague, she thought.[76] She gave descriptions of the Ethiopians she saw at Bure and Gore and was much impressed with the beauty of the countryside, (the Western

---

74 Bulpett, 102.
75 Bulpett, 101.
76 It was in fact to protect them from the Evil Eye.

Highlands are one of the most fertile parts of Ethiopia), all of which was duly quoted by Bulpett.

When they arrived at Gore, she tried to pay a courtesy call on the wife of Ras Tasamma,[77] who had come with his entourage to meet them at Gore. At first, despite the handsome gifts she sent - a cloak and a parasol - Lucie was refused an audience. Eventually after intervention by Harrington, Lucie was allowed to meet her. The Ras' wife turned out to be a disappointment and was described as very fat and not very black, and no conversation could be recorded, as she refused to admit the interpreter. A diplomatic incident was only just avoided.

The lively descriptions of Lucie McMillan's Ethiopian adventure then abruptly come to a halt. Whether she got her intended audience with the Empress Taitu is not recorded; we only know that she reached Addis Ababa, had an informal meeting with the emperor, and then returned via Dire Dawa to Jibuti.[78] It was an impressive journey for a woman in 1904 and showed she was a lady of considerable determination and independent character.

On April 9th Bulpett returned with the mules he had purchased in Gore and rejoined the others. By now the river was rising and the rainy season was approaching. Finally on April 29th they set out to march in the direction of Lake Rudolf, hoping to cover as yet unexplored and unmapped territory. The explorers Bottego and Austin had been some of the way but "had kept to the west of our route," according to Bulpett. He commented wryly that Jessen had a burning ambition to be an explorer and wanted to outdo Marchand.[79]

Their route was to take them south of the river Akobo, to map out the as yet unexplored plateau of Musha and then return via the Boma Plateau to Itang. With Ethiopia along one side and Kenya along the other, boundary questions were bound to arise in this remote corner

---

77 Ras Tasamma later became regent for Emperor Menelik II, after he was incapacitated by a stroke. He was a high-ranking imperial official, presumably sent to escort Harrington, the British Minister, into the capital.
78 "A St Louis Woman's Trip through Abyssinia," *St Louis Post-Dispatch*, 23 October 1904.
79 Bulpett, 92.

of Southern Sudan, which they did with frequency. In Northrup's time no government writ ran there. The area was sparsely inhabited by diverse tribes, who still lived as they always had done, undisturbed by European civilisation. It was a marvellous area for slavers and ivory poachers to hide from the arm of any law, especially in the rainy season when the plains became a morass and virtually inaccessible. It still is an area confusing to understand on modern maps and the fact that many of the names have changed in the last hundred years makes it even more difficult to follow exactly the route taken by the McMillan expedition. Technically according to the Menelik Boundary Commission, the land fell within Anglo-Egyptian Sudan, and as one of the last unexplored corners of Africa the expedition had high hopes they would be able to discover new, possibly important, information. Northrup wanted to go there as he had been told there were elephants and wonderful hunting.[80]

He found the usual large mammals, elephant, buffalo, leopard and cheetah, but no lion or rhino. The species in the area included the tiang, a sub species of the topi, the white-eared kob, a type of buck, and the Mongalla gazelle, similar to the Thomson's gazelle. All of these were shot and collected by Northrup as specimens for museums in England.

In 1904 no one had yet succeeded in reaching Lake Rudolf from the north. There had only been four expeditions which had reached the lake previous to this - those of Teleki, Donaldson Smith, Cavendish and Bottego, but they had approached it from different directions. The regions to the northwest of Lake Rudolf were still 'terra incognita' to Europeans. Captain M S Welby of the 18th Hussars had been across the Boma Plateau in 1898 and Major H H Austin and Major Gwynn, had led a survey party there in 1899-1900, but the McMillan expedition was hopeful of covering some entirely new ground.

---

80 Much of the Boma Plateau has now been made into a game park and is an extension of the Ethiopian Highlands. Inhabited by the Anuak, Murle, and Toposa tribes, it contains wetlands and birdlife. The Boma National Park, was established in 1986 and runs alongside the Gambela National Park in Ethiopia, both of which contain similar examples of wildlife.

A total of 120 men set off. This part of the expedition did not go well. The low-lying area between the Baro and Akobo rivers during the rainy season is full of small streams and riverbanks. The extremely heavy Northrup nearly had an accident as his unfortunate mule fell backwards while scaling a steep bank due to the weight on its back.[81] The condition of the pack mules deteriorated and many died. There was a mutiny of the Ethiopian porters and the perceived ringleader was flogged (shades of Stanley?). After this several porters understandably deserted, and there was then an acute shortage of men and provisions. Jessen doggedly continued with his meticulous surveys, Bulpett kept the discipline with difficulty, but it was clear that the whole expedition was in danger and they would have to turn back, unless a solution was found. By this time they had reached the Akobo and could see the mountainous country ahead, the object of their expedition.

In the end they agreed to split the group and only Bulpett and Jessen with the bulk of the remaining provisions and the strongest porters continued. Northrup stayed behind with Zaphiro and Marlow, who had been suffering from a severe ear infection, and led the remainder of the men back to camp at Itang and relative civilisation, hunting for the pot along the route.

Northrup with his great size and voracious appetite was never going to make the grade as a successful explorer. It was his out-of-control eating that severely depleted the stores in the first place, and the underfed Ethiopian mules could not carry his enormous weight. Just how do you tell your sponsor he is the nuisance (not his wife!) and is hampering the expedition? It must have been a considerable relief to the others, when he agreed to stay back.

The two Europeans and remaining 31 porters struggled on and succeeded in crossing the area of land between the Akoba and Lake Rudolf, but do not appear to have reached the lake itself. However, without an interpreter they experienced difficulties in communicating with the people they met and with little flour or rice their diet was miserable. An Ethiopian called Nuri, who had been acting as their

---

81 Bulpett, 133.

interpreter in the absence of Zaphiro, was sent to buy more flour, but never returned. A large part of the area surveyed turned out to be disappointing land unsuitable for agriculture. As soon as they judged their survey project to have been accomplished, they marched back to meet up with Northrup, who was waiting for them with very welcome provisions. They reached the camp at Pokum on July 1st.

The result as Bulpett grandly sums it up was this: "We passed through unexplored country, and procured data for defining a boundary line which would fix the limits of Abyssinia on its extreme south western border."[82] In the brief resume at the back of Bulpett's book it says:

> The expedition was organised by Mr McMillan to survey the Musha or Bome Plateau. The fact that one of the caravans marched 38 days on half rations, largely through a country flooded by incessant rain, shows that the excursion was very far from being a 'picnic.'

During the expedition Northrup had shot a great many wild animals and had collected a large number of skins and heads, which now needed to be treated and stowed into the launches. He had been asked to bring back a complete skeleton of a hippo, but after the bones were boiled and laid out to dry by their camp on the river at Pokum, a visiting jackal stole the bones! The hides all had to be first dried, then dowsed in kerosene and sprinkled with plenty of insect powder. Finally they were packed in airtight zinc-lined cases. It was a lengthy business, preserving the skins. Skulls needed boiling, but horns were simpler as they did not require much preparation. These precious trophies, evidence of his hunting prowess and adventure, would end up stuffed or mounted on wall plaques, in museums and in his homes on display.

The party eventually returned, towed by the mail steamer from Kodok. They survived a storm on the Nile, when their flotilla was hit by lightning and the barges with their precious cargo of trophies became detached and were driven onto the bank. It took 18 hours to get

---

82 Bulpett, 246.

them free. The remaining members of the expedition reached Cairo in mid-July, where McMillan, Marlow and Bulpett stayed on for a month, while Jessen returned to Norway.

As a result of this expedition, the main members, Bulpett, Jessen and Northrup, were made fellows of the Royal Geographical Society, an honour, which provided some compensation for their endeavours. Charles Bulpett remained for the rest of his life with the McMillans an indispensable part of the family. Northrup, however, lost interest in further exploration.[83]

---

83 William Northrup McMillan, Gentleman, was elected a fellow of the RGS on 8th May 1905. His proposers were Charles Bulpett and Robert Fairbanks. The reasons for his election were stated as: extensive exploration in North Eastern Central Africa, South Western Abyssinia. Sources of the Baro and Akobo rivers.

CHAPTER V

ARRIVAL IN BRITISH EAST AFRICA AND DECISION TO SETTLE.

Disappointed in his failure to shoot either rhino or lion on his recent expedition, Northrup with Bulpett, Marlow and a Dr Grote,[84] who joined them in Cairo, decided to go to British East Africa. British East Africa was reported to be wonderful shooting country with plenty of lions. They set off by ship to Mombasa in search of new hunting grounds and further adventures.

Coming from Egypt via Aden their ship made its way down the north coast of East Africa. The approach to Mombasa was a sight that could not fail to please. The old Portuguese fortress and white Arab buildings stood out in high relief against a background of lush vegetation of palms and banana trees and as the ship drew closer flowering bougainvillea and frangipani added splashes of colour to the view.

Northrup arrived off Kilindini, September 14th 1904. Kilindini harbour was at this date in its infancy, nothing like the major port it later became. Situated on the western side of Mombasa Island it was

84 A Dr De Groot is listed as a traveller in Stephen J North's List of Europeans in British Administered East Africa 1888-1905, which might possibly be the same man. Jessen comments that he was a keen photographer.

Northrup McMillan at the Mombasa Railway Station.

developed by the British because of its deep-water anchorage, which was more suited to large steamships than the old dhow harbour on the eastern side. When Northrup steamed in to Kilindini there was no infrastructure; ships anchored mid-stream and cargo was simply dumped on the beach and eventually placed in the single tin customs shed, while passengers were rowed ashore in little boats to the rudimentary landing jetty.

Northrup found the red tape at Mombasa irksome. Everyone was required to buy a licence of £50 in order to shoot game and another charge was levied on each of the firearms brought in; rifles, guns and revolvers. Only a limited amount of ammunition was allowed and Northrup, who had a veritable arsenal of weapons and way over the limit of ammunition, had a great deal of trouble with the authorities. Then his baggage was mislaid. After some argument and delay, it turned up in a far corner of the Customs Shed. He complained that everything was in a muddle and red tape was indulged to an exasperating extent. The four mules and two horses he had brought in from Aden were not allowed to go up country until they had been given a Mallein[85] Test, but there was no testing equipment available in Mombasa, so how could he comply with the rules? Eventually, after much protestation, he was given a special permit and was allowed to take his horses and mules as far as Athi.

No description survives of Northrup's first impressions of Mombasa, nor where he stayed while solving his difficulties in clearing customs and finding his lost luggage. The little we know about Northrup's first visit to British East Africa comes from Jessen's brief account included at the back of his book.

In 1904 there were few hotels in Mombasa, the most comfortable and probably the one chosen by Northrup, was the newly built Cecil, owned by M MacJohn.[86] This was situated opposite the Law Courts (opened in 1901), on the main road leading down to the sea front and the picturesque Portuguese Fort, known as Fort Jesus,[87] which was now being used as the local prison. The Cecil was a two-storied building

Mombasa in about 1904 with the Mombasa Club in the foreground.

85 This test was for glanders, an infectious, often fatal disease, that attacks the respiratory organs of horses, mules and donkeys and used to be endemic in Africa.
86 Mesrop Macjohn (1874-1915) was an Armenian trader, who began his career in Mombasa by running a provision store. He also owned the Masonic Hotel in Nairobi.
87 Now called Nkrumah Road. Neither the Castle nor the Metropole Hotel had been built and accommodation in Mombasa was still basic.

with amenities previously unseen in Mombasa. It had 18 bedrooms, baths with hot and cold water, a billiard room and a bar and advertised a service for meeting trains and boats.[88] Most importantly, it was within easy walking distance of Boustead and Ridley, The East African Stores, and other general agents and outfitters for up country travellers. The Mombasa Club, the social hub of European Mombasa, was also conveniently close.[89]

At this time European residents tended to stay at the Mombasa Club, while visiting officials would be put up by the Commissioner, or in his absence, the managing director of Smith Mackenzie Shipping Company, who had a house conveniently close to Kilindini, which was pleasantly spacious and breezy.

No doubt Northrup would have made use of the trolley service, hand pushed along a narrow gauge railway track laid along the main routes of the town, as Kilindini was about a mile distant from the centre of town. He would have visited the Old Town, still at this date the mercantile heart of Mombasa, with its Indian style shops and offices clustered close around the dhow harbour and just a few minutes walk from the Club. But Mombasa was changing fast and British style colonial offices and residences were springing up all over the island at an astonishing rate, submerging the old Afro-Arab character of Mombasa under a thin veneer of western civilisation.

Anxious to waste no time and escape the frustrations of bureaucracy, he caught the first available train to Nairobi. The Uganda Railway ran a bi-weekly service and went as far as Kisumu on Lake Victoria. Called the Lunatic Express, the railway had taken five years to build at enormous expense to British taxpayers, as well as costing many human lives. The line had been dug and the rails laid by thousands of Indian workmen brought in from India and the design was based on the railways in India. The first stage had been completed in 1901 and by 1904 most of the teething problems had been ironed out and the service was running well. First, second and third class tickets were offered and Northrup, like most Europeans, travelled first class. The first class carriages were

88 E.A. Handbook, 1909.
89 Founded in 1897.

A cartoon of the 'Lunatic Line' railway in the early days.

simple wooden boxes on wheels with room for four passengers per compartment. There were no corridors and the sides were of a slatted construction to allow ventilation. Though not nearly as luxurious as the American railroads Northrup grew up with, the Uganda Railway served its purpose well. Nairobi could now be reached within two days. The foot caravans that had previously struggled through the Taru desert had taken weeks or even months to reach their destination. African and Indian traders as well as Europeans benefited from the railway. Trade goods and provisions could now be transported with far greater ease. Ivory could be carried to the coast by rail, rather than by slaves chained together. Indian entrepreneurs could run business empires stretching from Uganda to the Coast, government officials could administrate with greater efficiency.

The railway transported many settlers to a new life in East Africa and the scenes these newcomers saw from the train windows often remained memorable for many years to come. The train left Mombasa station at five in the evening, roughly two hours before dusk, when the temperature was pleasantly cool after the heat of the day. The train was provided with two engines as the journey was uphill all the way. The ride was hardly a luxury experience, and Northrup, the railway specialist, was not impressed. At certain stages the lines were so uneven and the carriages rattled so much that it was recommended that passengers who had false teeth remove them, while goggles were needed to protect the eyes from the red dust that blew in from the Taru plains covering travellers from head to foot. The windows had rolling blinds of mosquito gauze, which could be lowered when the windows were open. These had the added function of providing protection from the soot and flying sparks from the engines. Just outside Mombasa the train slowed at Changamwe and children ran along the line offering mangoes, pineapples and other fruits to the passengers through the windows. Further along at Samburu, travellers could get out and stretch their legs, while coal and water was taken on. At Voi the train stopped at the Dak bungalow for an evening meal and first class passengers were served with watery soup, stewed beef and cabbage, followed by tinned fruit and custard, liberally encrusted with flying insects. Later they sat on the veranda and smoked while their bedrolls were laid out and the oil lamps lit by the railway staff who scrambled along the tops of the carriages opening the flaps to reach the lights with long tapers. Northrup, the gourmet, did not enjoy the meal he was served and complained that his bedding had bedbugs and was none too clean. He recommended strongly that passengers take their own bedding and food with them, when travelling on the train.

The next morning when he woke up he could feel the rise in altitude and change from the humid air of the coast. He drew up the blinds and looked out and saw Mount Kilimanjaro soaring in the distance and the wild animals thick on the Athi plains. His excitement grew and he forgot all his trials and declared British East Africa to be "the greatest game country in the world." At this period train schedules were not exact as the train would often stop at a passenger's request if they wished to take a pot shot at animals seen along the way, or to admire a spectacular view. Some engines had a cowcatcher seat at the front, where favoured passengers were allowed to sit. It took Northrup 36 hours to reach Nairobi and he arrived on September 24th and stayed for the first week at the Masonic

Hotel.

On reaching Nairobi Northrup looked round the town. He called it 'Tinsville' due to all the roofs made of that material. One of the first things he did was to pay courtesy calls on the Commissioner and Sub Commissioner.

The Commissioner was the newly appointed Sir Donald Stewart. He had replaced Sir Charles Eliot in August, 1904. Sir Donald was a military man with a fondness for alcohol, who has been unflatteringly described as "lacking business experience or training except perhaps in the racing world. He rarely read files and as he went late to bed and rose late in the morning the affairs of the country received scant attention."[90] But

he knew that one of his main priorities was to encourage the economic development of the Protectorate in order to make the railway profitable, and when Northrup came to see him, a man with a large amount of money and excellent connections, he was at his most flattering and accommodating.

The Sub-Commissioner was Frederick Jackson (1860-1929) who had first arrived in East Africa in 1884 and was originally employed by the IBEACo[91] before transferring his services to HM Government. He was

Charles Bulpett (left) with Northrup on their first hunting trip to Kenya in 1904. Kikuyu men are in the foreground.

90 Charles Hobley, *From Chartered company to Crown Colony* (1929), 127.
91 Imperial British East Africa Company (1888-95), which ran East Africa on a private basis in much the same way as the former British East India Company. However it was singularly unsuccessful and never made a profit and in 1895 control was passed to the Foreign Office.

an 'old Africa hand,' a traveller and fellow big game hunter and must have been a useful and pleasant contact for Northrup to meet on his arrival in Nairobi.

Northrup was assigned a plot on a farm in Nderugu to pitch his camp. This farm was called Long JuJu[92] and it belonged to a Major Ringer, who

The original farmhouse at Long Juju.

had served in the army in West Africa. It was situated in a valley not far from the Athi River, next to the Nderugu River, close to Ol Donyo Sabuk. Northrup was entranced by the hunter's paradise he found. Jessen tells us that Ol Donyo Sabuk, a small hump-shaped mountain, which was the only high ground in the surrounding plains, was at that time owned by five or six Englishmen. They had formed a syndicate to protect the game on it, particularly the buffalo. The mountain was covered with grass from top to bottom, but near the top and in all the valleys and ravines were dense forests, frequented by different varieties of game and a herd of buffalo, the only herd existing in the neighbourhood. From the top there were wonderful views across the surrounding countryside. Towards the north could be seen the snow-capped peaks of Mount Kenya. Due west the tin roofs of Nairobi glittered in the sun and to the south the magnificent Athi plains rolled out seemingly to infinity. The nearby river had hippos and plentiful amounts of fish and the picturesque waterfalls and running rivulets presented an idyllic picture.

92 Elwood Taylor, personal interview. Major Charles Harding Newman Ringer (1860-1913) served in West Africa, fought in the infamous Sack of Benin, and in the Boer War. He then worked for the Cape Government Railway before coming to East Africa. A keen big game hunter and part-time farmer, he jointly owned the Norfolk Hotel, which opened on Christmas Day 1904, and was to become the chief watering hole and meeting place for Europeans in Nairobi. He became a good friend of Northrup's and on one occasion went to America with him. He died in a yachting accident in Falmouth.

Northrup

John Boyes was assigned to the party as the professional hunter and guide. John Boyes (1873-1951) like Jackson came originally from Yorkshire, England. He had arrived in East Africa in 1898 and was a trader by profession. In 1900 he was charged with illegal trading, and sent for trial in Mombasa, but was eventually acquitted. Known as King of the Wa-Kikuyu, he knew the people and the country well and was the ideal man to show a newcomer around.

The party proceeded to enjoy excellent hunting. Northrup shot his rhino and Bulpett had a close shave with a lion. His first shot had merely stunned the animal, who had laid down as if dead, but when Bulpett approached, the lion recovered and sprang up and knocked him to the ground, but not before Bulpett had fired another shot. Fortunately this time the lion was mortally wounded. But Bulpett, badly shaken, scrambled away and climbed up a nearby thorn tree, waiting there until he was certain the lion was really dead. His gunbearer was injured and Bulpett was scratched mainly by his encounter with the thorn bush rather than the lion. His sun helmet received an impressive dent and he kept it as a relic of his lion hunt.

Northrup liked the place so much he decided not to go with the others to Uganda. Instead he pleaded poor health and stayed behind in Nairobi and spent his time inspecting land with a view to purchasing a site for a cattle ranch and was successful in purchasing 10,000 acres 20 miles east of Nairobi adjacent to Major Ringer's land. He also found time to have his photograph taken by W D Young, the leading photographer in town. The picture entitled W N McMillan Esquire, 1904, shows Northrup, cigarette casually in hand, posed on a studio bench.

On 9th January 1905 Northrup

A photographic portrait of Northrup McMillan in 1904.

returned to the Coast and proceeded to Cairo, where he briefly met up with Jessen. Jessen had delivered three new boats to Khartoum, ordered by Northrup from Norway, and was fully expecting Northrup to join him on another attempt to navigate the Blue Nile.[93] Mr L C Scott, an American chemist and assayer, who Northrup had employed to look at the gold deposits along the Blue Nile, had also arrived in Cairo. However, Northrup was no longer interested in exploring the Blue Nile. He had moved on; his Kenya project was his new enthusiasm and occupied all his energies. When Jessen and Scott met him in Cairo Jan 28th-30th, 1905, Northrup excused himself, saying he had agreed to meet his wife in Spain and was not feeling up to the rigours of another expedition.

Jessen, however, a most tenacious Norwegian, was determined to hold Northrup to his word. In the end it was agreed that Jessen and Scott would go alone, and Northrup would foot the bill.

The second Blue Nile expedition was gruelling, for when navigation became impossible Jessen and Scott attempted to walk along the riverbed and the banks of the Blue Nile with a mule caravan.

View of Ol Donyo Sabuk with campsite.

[93] These boats were designed by Colin Archer of Larvik, who had built Nansen's boat *Fram,* as used on his polar expedition, as it was hoped they would prove more suited to the river conditions than the previous ones.

Scott became extremely ill and almost died. Little was achieved as the gold he found was in insufficient quantities to be economically viable. They were arrested at one point, despite carrying special passes from Kitchener's successor, Reginald Wingate, the British Governor in Sudan and from Emperor Menelik of Ethiopia.

They got as far as Burie, when the river finally defeated them and they climbed out and continued their journey across country on foot. The two explorers arrived at Addis Ababa more dead than alive.[94]

After finishing his business in Cairo, Northrup returned to London, where he had agreed to meet Lucie and travel to Spain together. She had gone to America with John Destro and Louise Decker after her Ethiopian adventure, but was now waiting for her husband in England.

In September 1905 Northrup was back once again in Nairobi, having ordered a bungalow in parts and all kinds of equipment to set up his cattle ranch.[95] He managed to buy more land including Major Ringer's farm, Long Juju. Major Ringer had newly opened The Norfolk Hotel and needed the money, so was willing to sell.

An idea of the living conditions and hardships of the early settler's first farming ventures in Kenya can be imagined from this amusing tale of Major Ringer and his horse.

At that time it was no unusual thing for lions to sit in a row outside one's door by night and roar. The settler thinks no more of this than he would of barking dogs, unless he cannot sleep for the noise, when he goes to the edge of the yard and shoos them away. Major Ringer's favourite horse had a habit of poking his nose out of the high open window above his stall. One night an inquisitive lion crawled up to the window and sat licking his chops beneath it, when he saw the nose

94 It was not until 1968 that the course of the Blue Nile was at last successfully followed the whole way. This was done at the request of Emperor Haile Selassie, by a British and Ethiopian military team lead by colonel John Blashford-Snell.
95 "Mr McMillan, Jessen, Bayliss, Kay, Marlow, Towell arrived in Port Said by P&O SS Osiris and leave the 4th of next month on P & O SS Persia for Aden en route to Mombasa. Mr McMillan's intention is to open up quite a new colony." Newspaper cutting from W N McMillan Scrapbooks RH, Micr.Afr.641.

getting its airing. Rising on his hind legs, the lion made a swipe at the nose with his big fore paw. The sharp claws raked the horse's face from the eyes down to the sensitive nostrils, drawing blood and sending the horse into hysterics, not so much for the pain as the sudden whiff he got of lion odour. The screams of the horse put the lion to startled flight and awakened the Major. Nothing would induce the horse again to enter the stable after nightfall, so the major installed the horse in the house and went to sleep himself in the stable. This was the state of things at Long Juju, when McMillan took possession and renovated the premises.'[96]

Northrup then acquired the mountain, Ol Donyo Sabuk, from the syndicate, bringing his total land ownership up to 20,000 acres causing Jessen to comment dryly that Mr McMillan now had his own game park. He wrote that his employer was busying himself making the farm comfortable for the visit of Mrs McMillan and Charles Bulpett who were due out early in 1906. The farm was to be supplied with a refrigeration plant, electric light, blacksmith shop, water tower, stables, stores, dairy, etc. The long-suffering Jessen was employed to oversee the shipping of all the necessary equipment, while a Mr W Bayliss had been taken on as Manager and General Engineer and a Mr Kay as the electrical engineer.

The McMillan Party enjoyed more successful hunting in the New Year, and Lucie McMillan succeeded in shooting a huge lion with a black mane, (usually only found in the Maasai Mara). The last picture of the Jessen book shows Lucie's lion, stuffed and in ferocious pose, standing in the hall of the McMillan's new London House, 19 Hill Street, Berkeley Square, W1 in the heart of fashionable Mayfair.

Jessen, the Norwegian engineer and cartographer, had hoped to be involved in some serious exploration but must have been disappointed with his employer. He had great admiration for Lucie. "It makes a man hold his breath with wonder and admiration for a lady possessed of

96 T R MacMechen, "Juja Ranch, British East Africa Big Game Hunting," *Mc-Clure's Magazine* (March 1909).

such undaunted nerve and pluck as that displayed by Mrs McMillan,"[97] he gushed, but had little to say about Northrup, complimentary or otherwise. While he described Lucie as a crack shot, he remains silent about Northrup's prowess in that direction, despite the large numbers of animals he killed. Jessen was in the pay of Northrup so he couldn't say what he thought. But working for a millionaire playboy had its drawbacks. It does not appear that anything significant was achieved from any of the enormously expensive expeditions and once Northrup discovered Kenya (or British East Africa as it should be called at this time) he never went back to Sudan or Ethiopia. Jessen and his millionaire parted company, after the book was written.[98]

Conditions in British East Africa of 1905 exactly suited Northrup. It reminded him of his romantic ideal of the Wild West before it was tamed and of New Mexico and its cowboys. Instead of Native Indians, there were the Maasai and other African tribes. The climate and altitude was good for his health, while the vast open plains teeming with wildlife was his idea of heaven.

The early settlers and the officials he met were his kind of people,

Moving equipment to the farm at Juja.

---

97 Jessen, 403.
98 Lucie appears to have taken an interest in Jessen and helped him produce the book. She supplied many of the photographs, while Jessen did the excellently detailed drawings and maps.

active outdoors men, straightforward guys who enjoyed a drink and a hearty meal afterwards and perhaps some horseplay when somewhat merry. Nairobi was a one-horse town, but no worse than towns Northrup had seen out West and the railway, which had spawned Nairobi in the first place, was very familiar.

Northrup arrived at a time when conditions were favourable for a man like him, able and willing to invest. In 1904/5 land could be bought easily and cheaply. The railway had been completed at great cost by the British taxpayer and now the 'powers that be' at home were demanding some evidence that their great undertaking had been worthwhile. Settlers, working farms and businesses were desperately needed for the colonization process to begin. What was the point of a railway, if there were no goods and people to transport?

Kenya was unusual in that a Colonial Administration was put in place before the bulk of settlers came. The usual course of events was for settlers or colonizers to arrive first and a government to slowly evolve afterwards, but in Kenya it happened in reverse. Laws and rules had already been formulated and the settlers found themselves on arrival restricted by bureaucracy and red tape. The land laws were particularly confusing, as no decision had been made on the ultimate goal for Kenya. Was it the intention that the Protectorate become a White Man's land like Australia or America, or was it to remain African, where the rights of the natives remained paramount and the land was governed on behalf of the African population? No clear policy was formulated until much later. To begin with it was extremely difficult to get any land at all as there were no guidelines as to how the land should be allotted or where settlement should be allowed. Officials did not want to commit themselves to handing out plots of land that were not viable or belonged to someone else.

At the beginning of the 20th century the Kikuyu people were in poor shape, decimated by drought, disease and the raids of the Maasai. The Government surveyors mistook the situation and thought the empty land they saw in Kikuyu was there for the taking and as no objections were raised allowed settlement to take place. It was the Maasai, being at that point in ascendance, whom they recognised as the dominant tribe, and with whom they made their early treaties. The British early on acknowledged an existence of exclusive Maasai country and no settlement was allowed in those areas, but other tribes were not treated with as much respect.

Lord Delamere was one of the first settlers, who managed to get a government grant of 100,000 acres in the Rift Valley, between Njoro and the Molo River in 1903. The land was held on a 99 years' lease at an annual rent of £200 and Delamere bound himself to spend £5,000 (a large sum of money in those days) in development within five years. He only got it because the land was absolutely unoccupied and no question of native rights arose. The officials thought he was quite mad to want it. His previous applications for more suitable farming land at Laikipia and Naivasha had been refused.

Sir Charles Eliot, the first Commissioner of British East Africa, was instructed initially to encourage more settlement by giving out generous leases of land of up to 640 acres for farms in carefully selected areas where there appeared to be no conflict of interest, or native settlement or grazing grounds. Delamere helped him publicise the settlement drive in England. In September 1903 Sir Charles Eliot sent his Commissioner of Customs, Mr A Marsden, down to South Africa to advertise the new land grants there. The response from South Africa was much greater than had been anticipated and it overwhelmed the system. Early in 1904 hundreds of South Africans turned up in Nairobi demanding homesteads. But not enough farms had been set aside and surveyed. There was a general panic. Alarmed by such demand, Government policies suddenly changed and became obstructive. The land office was set up and more delays occurred as title deeds were drawn up and officials dragged their feet in true bureaucratic style. These stop and go policies, as they were called, were very frustrating for those who came expecting land. There were stories of would-be settlers waiting for the land leases they had been promised, giving up because of the wait. Sometimes they ran out of money and lost their deposits from having to pay living costs during the long wait in Nairobi.

As Elspeth Huxley explains in her biography of Lord Delamere, settlers had to protest hard to get the access to the land, labour and transport they wanted to make the colony a profitable venture. It was a struggle both against seemingly unsympathetic officialdom and the vagaries of disease and unknown conditions in an untried land.

Sir Charles Eliot (1862-1931) was Commissioner of British East Africa from 1900-1904. He was a scholarly and intelligent man, a specialist in sea slugs, and an effective administrator. He resigned on a matter of principle in June 1904 after a dispute with the Foreign Secretary, Lord Lansdowne. This was because the Foreign Office had ordered him go back on his word and refuse a lease of 50 square miles to a private individual, which he had already agreed upon. This he refused to do as he considered the instruction unjust, especially as the Government had recently waived through an application for 500 square miles to a syndicate of businessmen. He tendered his resignation, which was accepted, and he returned to England. Sir Donald Stewart (1860-1905) was sent out to replace him. He was not an able administrator, nor a good choice to head the newest British colonial acquisition. He died just over a year later of alcohol poisoning and during his tenure the policy of drift, as it is politely called, got considerably worse. In April 1905 control of the protectorate was transferred from the Foreign Office to the Colonial Office and a firmer grip was taken by the home government.

One of the first settlers Northrup met in Nairobi was Ewart Grogan and the two men became good friends. Ewart Grogan (1874-1967) had arrived in Kenya in 1904 shortly before Northrup. He had gone into partnership with a South African called Lingham and was looking at the possibility of extracting timber along the railway. To do this he wanted to purchase a large acreage of forest. Initially he was promised this by Commissioner Stewart, but later difficulties arose. He also took the opportunity of buying parcels of land in Nairobi and Mombasa, which were on cheap offer and Northrup went in with him.

Ewart Grogan was a household name at this time. His Cape to Cairo trek had made him world famous. It was a most romantic and daring undertaking, for it was claimed that he had walked the length of Africa in order to win the hand of his bride Gertrude Watt, a wealthy heiress from New Zealand. Northrup was living in England when Grogan arrived back in March 1900 and addressed the Royal Geographical Society and may well have first met him there. It was in fact Rhodes, whose dream of a Cape to Cairo railway and telegraph route had actually inspired Grogan to undertake the trek, but the silver tongued Grogan, ever the self publicist, knew how to captivate an audience.

Grogan and Northrup had much in common. They had similar interests, were from similar backgrounds and were close in age. They were both wealthy sons of successful businessmen unlike Lord Delamere (1870-1931) who, though a couple of years older than Northup, was an aristocrat. Grogan's father was an estate agent in London. Both men were interested in Big Game Hunting and Exploration in Africa. Grogan like Northrup had been fascinated by Africa from an early age after reading Selous and Rider Haggard's *King Solomon's Mines*. Northrup, the would-be African explorer, admired Grogan for his successful and adventurous experiences, and was influenced by his ideas. Grogan was a clever and handsome man with an eye for the ladies and a gift of the gab, and he rose to prominence early on as a natural leader of the East African Settlers. Grogan's 'go-getting' attitude made him popular with the early pioneering group, but after WW1 his star began to wane.

Edward Paice, Grogan's biographer, complained that Elspeth Huxley airbrushed Grogan out of her book on Lord Delamere and the history of white settlement, and did not give him the importance he deserved. By the 1930s, when Huxley wrote her seminal account, Grogan had fallen out of favour. He had been in prison and was a serial adulterer. Elspeth Huxley disapproved of him. He was always quarrelling with the authorities – picking holes in the administration – but like Delamere he did a great deal for the development of Kenya. There was a certain amount of competition between the two men. Paice relates an incident when Delamere said he wanted to try out pig farming, while Grogan said he would introduce trout to see how they did in the streams on Mount Kenya. Both flourish today, so the rivalry between the two men benefited Kenya! Grogan's private wharf at Mbaraki so annoyed the authorities that it stimulated them into getting their act together, finally building the port at Kilindini and eventually purchasing Mbaraki from him.

Kenya was a sportsman's heaven and Northrup, a connoisseur of sporting entertainments, was in his element. The races were an important social event in Nairobi and in the early life of the Protectorate. Twice a year, at Christmas and in July, settlers would converge on Nairobi for the race weeks. It was an excuse for all kinds of parties and drunken revels. There was flamboyant and eccentric dress, with wild evenings, and impromptu dances. The East African Turf Club started by A S Cooper in 1900, was taken seriously with racehorses owned by wealthy owners and bloodstock bred and trained locally. Cups were presented and bets changed hands.

It was also a chance for hardworking settlers to let off steam, to meet each other, to do some networking and forget about their farming worries. The Edwardian character of the pre-war period, with its emphasis on public schoolboy horseplay and hard drinking men behaving badly seems to have suited Northrup. It was the kind of society he understood. There was an innocence and a brashness in the early part of the century, people had faith, they believed it was all worth while and that they were helping to build up a new British colony and were taking part in a great adventure.

Perhaps in the early years before he became too fat Northrup might have indulged in fox hunting and played cricket – two very British sports, which were quickly imported to the colony – and polo, which had been introduced from India.

The Masara pack of hounds had their kennels just outside Nairobi, and the master was Mr Jim Elkington. The only difference being that instead of a fox, a jackal or a duiker was hunted. The meet was held at dawn as the scent only lay on the ground when the grass was wet with dew. Otherwise all was the same as in England with red coats, huntsmen's caps and the horn to call the hounds.

Kenya was indeed a sportsman's paradise. All these activities could be enjoyed with a wonderful freedom, and at much less cost and inconvenience than in the old country.

Then there was the cult of the Noble Savage; the Maasai and Somali, were especially admired for their nomadic life style, living wild and free. They were considered to be a cut above the other African tribes and idealised for their proud and noble bearing. Somalis were often employed as head servants and attired in a long white robe and a red fez they looked suitably grand. Lord Delamere was the champion of the Maasai. He tried to give them special treatment and favoured the creation of Native Reserves, where tribes could live life as they always had done, under their own chiefs separate from the colonists, who had different rules and regulations. This arrangement had similarities with the American solution, but just as in America it did not ultimately work. The special treatment given to the Maasai proved disadvantageous to them in the long run. The need for labour and security undermined the independence of the reserves and WWI proved to be the turning point.

While nowadays the racist views of the early settlers would be viewed with horror, in the early 1900s it was the accepted norm. There was a casual racism, with no thought or bad intention behind it. It was just accepted, much in the same way as the settlers accepted the servants they had and the rigid divisions between the classes. It was a fact of life and viewed rather like the Indian caste system, as part of a structured society where each had their place and part to play. Those with the benefits of inherited wealth understood the responsibility that came with it and often took on the mantle of leadership and gave help to the poor and needy. The lower mostly accepted their position as preordained in the natural order of things and women, in the pre-feminist age, by and large accepted a supportive role and did not claim equality with their husbands. The concept of multi-culturalism, of all people and races being equal, was beyond their imagination and the possibility of Africa having independent democratic governments, run on the same lines as their own in Britain or America, was to them simply pie in the sky.

Elspeth Huxley,[99] who was born in 1907 to a settler family, understood the views and beliefs of the early colonists in Kenya and explains them well: Settlement was viewed as part of a cultural conviction. There was the so-called 'Dual Mandate,' whereby a colonising power had a duty to develop the resources of the country over which it had control to the maximum extent in the interests of everybody. The pioneer settler was seen as a benefactor, as by adding to a country's wealth he was adding also to everyone's prosperity. This was the justification for moving on to land, which he could put to better economic use than its previous owners. There was a theory of 'beneficial occupation of land,' whereby land should be used by the man who could turn it to the greatest productivity and conversely it was wrong to leave potential agricultural land unoccupied and uncultivated. Now that the world is surfeited and does not need more cultivation or more population, it is a difficult viewpoint to take on board, but in the early 20th century the vast tracts of 'under-utilised' land in Africa seemed to provide a solution to a universal shortage.

Another inherent conviction held by the early settlers was that western civilisation was a good thing. They believed in a definite Right and Wrong, and did not doubt that it was better to be Civilised than Savage. Anyone who spread western civilisation was doing right, was conferring a benefit on the people he helped to civilise.

> 'To suggest that the interests of the natives were paramount would have seemed to that generation a mere contradiction in terms. The idea that the interests of an assortment of barbaric, ideal less and untutored tribesmen, clothed in sheep's fat, castor oil or rancid butter, men who smelt out witches, drank blood warm from the throats of living cattle and believed that rainfall depended on the arrangement

---

99 Elspeth Huxley died in 1997 aged 89. She wrote several books about conditions in colonial Kenya, including her well known *Flame Trees of Thika, Memories of an African childhood* (1959), which tells the story of her mother Nellie Grant and her own experiences as a pioneer settler.

of a goats intestines should be exalted above those of the educated European would have seemed to them fantastic'[100]

---

100 Elspeth Huxley, *Lord Delamere and the Making of Kenya* (1953 edition), 81.

CHAPTER VI

JUJA
'THE FINEST SPORTING ESTATE IN THE WORLD'[101]

Juja was the ultimate embodiment of Northrup's African dream. It was his personal creation into which he put his heart and soul, and it is the place most closely associated with his memory. Conceived primarily as a place to view animals and enjoy the hunting experience rather than as a working farm, it was the first of its kind in Kenya and was instrumental in promoting the fashion for safari tourism. With its home comforts and plentiful wildlife within easy access, it was a forerunner of present day safari game parks with their hotel-style lodges, catering to every need. The idea was not original as Juja was modelled on the old shooting lodges and sporting estates owned by wealthy aristocratic families, which Northrup would have visited in Scotland and Europe. But transposed into a different landscape with exotic African animal life, and on a much larger and luxurious scale, Northrup created at Juja a unique experience that impressed all who visited.

   As usual Northrup was ahead of his time. His hope that the colonial

101 This phrase appears on the front cover of the elaborate sales brochure put out by Newland Tarlton & Company. Many of the descriptions of Juja in this chapter come from this source which was kindly lent to me by Johnnie Nettlefold grandson of Frederick Nettlefold, who bought Juja Estate in 1921.

A newspaper depiction of McMillan's Juja Estate.

government would sanction his idea for a game reserve and zoological garden on the doorstep of Nairobi did not materialise. In 1910 he had planned to amalgamate with his neighbour Hugh Heatley,[102] who owned Kamiti ranch, and create a huge swathe of parkland set aside for hunting safaris, to be called Juja Hunters Club, but the scheme flopped. The colonial government saw no benefit in recreation grounds for sportsmen. They could not see into the future or imagine a time when mass tourism and national parks would provide valuable sources of income.

Juja acquired its romantic reputation from descriptions of safaris in literary accounts, and glowing reports brought back by visitors. Many early travellers to Kenya, hunted at Juja and either camped on the McMillan land or stayed at his house. More than 10,000 head of game roamed freely over the estate, which included the mountain Ol Donyo Sabuk. All the main species of East African wildlife were represented there, apart from elephant. The rare roan antelope lived on the mountain with a herd of buffalo and lions were plentiful on the

---

102 Hugh Heatley had also arrived in East Africa in 1904. Initially he stayed as a guest of Lord Delamere but was so impressed with the country that he decided to purchase land of his own.

113

plains. As every hunter wanted to shoot lion, at just over 20 miles from the centre of Nairobi, Juja was a favoured starting off point for hunting expeditions.

Edward Stewart White,[103] an American writer, who wrote books on sporting travel and adventure, visited in 1912. He devoted a chapter of his book, *Land of Footprints,* published in 1913, to Juja. In it he described how Juja Farm loomed up unexpectedly from the rolling plains, a white shimmering structure set about with numerous outbuildings, suddenly appearing on the horizon amidst the endless expanse of grassy landscape thick with wild animals. Approached by a long slanting drive, it was a place of unbelievable luxury with hot baths, electric lights and abundant food and drink. After a long hard trek and nights spent under canvas, it seemed like a mirage seen in the desert, an oasis too miraculous to be real.

Guests sat on the wide verandas shaded by climbing vines, cooled by the manicured gardens surrounding the house. A megaphone and a huge telescope on a tripod stood in one corner. There were pictures

on the walls and rugs on the floor. Here they recounted their adventures and relived the excitement of the hunt, comfortably seated in wicker chairs with extending footrests. Well-trained servants dressed in long white robes brought in trays of iced and fizzy

An early view of Juja Farmhouse, showing the kitchen extension at the back and the ladders to the attic, where safari equipment was stored.

drinks in thin glasses. Afterwards, in the dining room, laid with white napery, glittering with silver and glass and bright with flowers, a dinner of several courses followed ending with black coffee, shelled nuts and candied fruit.

It was very much a man's place and Lucy never liked Juja. She disapproved of the raucous parties and hunters' jamborees and would

103 Edward Stewart White (1873- 1946) was an outdoorsman originally from Michigan.

The bachelor's quarters at Juja.

disappear to a nearby bungalow for some peace and quiet while her husband held noisy court until the early hours of the morning. There was a bachelor's mess provided next to the main homestead where an overflow of Northrup's hunting guests could stay.

This had six bedrooms and a large communal dining room decorated with stuffed heads, like a clubhouse. Quite frequently hunting expeditions would come through with written permission to stay at Juja even though the owner was not in residence. The staff would be waiting, the table laid, the beds turned down – reminiscent of the modern safari experience. Northrup was a famously generous host and kept open house at Juja. His hospitality was legendary, even at a time when hospitality to passing travellers was very much the norm in Kenya.

In 1905 Northrup had constructed his Juja House, rather like an Ikea flat-pack. It was made from panels of Uralite, an early type of asbestos sheeting, which was laid on a steel framework raised from the ground on iron piles. It was a simple barn-like structure with a steep roof with wide wooden verandas attached, which went all the way round the building. At the back a kitchen was connected to the house by a passage, in the typical fashion of early colonial houses. The roof space, reached by an exterior ladder, had ample room for gun racks and camping equipment.

All the building materials had to be transported by bullock cart

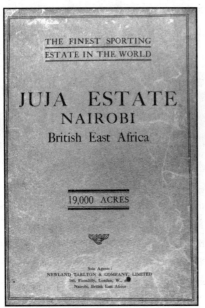

THE FINEST SPORTING
ESTATE IN THE WORLD

JUJA ESTATE
NAIROBI
British East Africa

19,000 ACRES

Sole Agents:
NEWLAND TARLTON & COMPANY, LIMITED
166, Piccadilly, London, W.
Nairobi, British East Africa

Front cover of the sales brochure
for McMillan's Estate at Juja.

from the railhead in Nairobi, and the road cleared as they moved along. The site chosen for the house stood on a slight ridge near the junction of the Nairobi and Rueru (now Ruiru) rivers on the edge of the Athi Plains. The land had been purchased, as was standard, on a 99-year lease, with a ground rent of half a pence per acre, paid annually to the Crown or colonial government as it later became. The owner was required by law to construct his own road to the property and then develop the land within a certain time frame or forfeit it.

It was a challenging undertaking and Northrup threw himself into the task with his customary enthusiasm. Everything was to be on the grand scale, with no expense spared and every eventuality catered for.

The main house had five bedrooms, a drawing room, a dining room, bathroom, kitchen, pantries, large attic and all conveniences, including electric light, water laid on to every bedroom and a sewage system. Next door there was a manager's bungalow with three bedrooms, a two-bed bungalow (Lucie's bolthole) and three other bungalows housing the post and telegraph office, chauffeurs and gardeners. Then there was the guesthouse or Bachelor's Mess as already described. There was a stone dairy for cheese and butter making, a stone slaughterhouse, a store, servants' quarters with 12 rooms, stables with accommodation for 26 horses, a coach house, barn and separate harness room. There were cattle yards and sheds for 700 head of cattle, garages, an incubator house, lion cages, carpentry shops, poultry runs and pigeon lofts, beautiful avenues and well laid out gardens all encompassed in a compound of 40 acres, with water laid on everywhere by means of a dam and water-

A later view of the Juja Farmhouse showing the gardens leading down to the Ruera River.

A view of Juja House taken in 2011.

The end view of Juja House taken in 2011. The kitchen extension is just visible on the left.

tower. An engine house provided power for the lighting, saw bench and an ice plant. Below the house stretched an irrigated fruit and vegetable garden with oranges, lemons, paw paws, pineapples, bananas and all kinds of vegetables.[104]

Four miles away on the banks of the Ndurugu River was Long Juju, Major Ringer's original farm, where Northrup had camped on his first visit in 1904. The simple hut-like dwelling, where Major Ringer had lived with his horse, was converted into a roomy bungalow for control of the northern part of the Estate complete with ostrich sheds and cattle bomas. There was road and telephone connection to Juja central.[105]

As the 1921 sales brochure rightly said there was no other farm in BEA so highly

---

104 Juja House still exists in its original form and is privately owned by the Harries family, but all the wild animals have gone and the estate has now been subdivided for building plots. Most of the outlying buildings have also disappeared.
105 Edward Stewart White, *Land of Footprints* (1912). William Marlow, Northrup's former footman and personal servant, managed Long Juju in 1912.

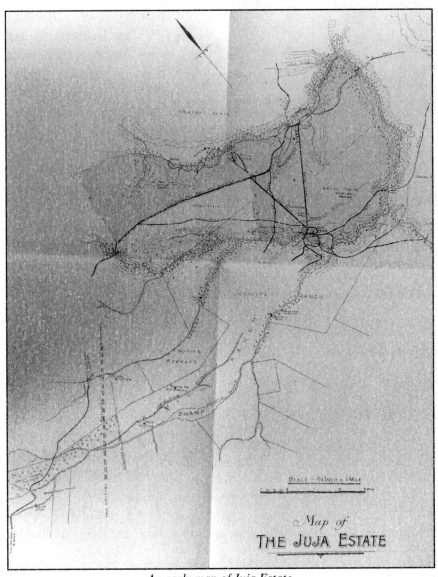

An early map of Juja Estate.

Louise Decker on the steps at Juja. Note the iron piles and panel construction.

Lucie McMillan on horseback with Juja house in the background.

improved as Juja. Amply watered by the Rueru, Ndurugu and Athi rivers, the land consisted of grazing grounds and river flats. There were wattle plantations and fruit gardens and maize fields on the river flats, but the property was pre-eminently a stock farm.

By the time Northrup had finished building and buying up available land, Juja had expanded far beyond his original intentions. It had become like a small village or an enormous English country house estate, but set in Africa and created in a few short years, rather than evolved over centuries. There were continual new additions and experiments, which required an ever-greater workforce to service. But though self sufficient in all its amenities, Juja never turned in a profit for its owner. Northrup, the bon viveur and generous host, who liked to impress and have the company of good cheer around him, was not a businessman at heart. He poured huge amounts of money into his favourite project, but it proved a bottomless pit, requiring ever more. He tried to raise sheep, ostrich and cattle, but only the cattle proved relatively successful. Under the McMillan stewardship Juja remained a haven for wildlife, a rich man's playground, where Northrup could relax in the company of his friends in the environment he enjoyed.

Theodore Roosevelt, the ex-president of America, was undoubtedly Juja's most famous and influential visitor.[106] Roosevelt is credited with popularising the term safari[107] as it is customarily used today. After his visit the safari craze caught on, and travel to Kenya, especially from America, increased dramatically.

In March 1909, shortly after the end of his presidency, Roosevelt embarked on a leisurely visit to Europe and East and Central Africa. Financed by Andrew Carnegie and by his own proposed writings, Roosevelt's party proposed to hunt for specimens for the Smithsonian

106 Theodore Roosevelt (1858-1919) was the 26th President of America serving from 1902-1909.
107 Safari is a Swahili word simply meaning journey and was in everyday use long before it was picked up on by the European travelling fraternity. The encyclopaedia now defines safari as a distinctive way of hunting – consisting of several days or weeks journey camping in the bush or jungle, while pursuing big game. The hunter is usually accompanied by a professional hunter, local guides, skinners, porters, etc.

St Louis newspapers ran articles about Roosevelt's upcoming safari.

Institute and for the American Museum of Natural History in New York. Following the fashion of former hunter explorers, his trip was styled as a scientific expedition. Three naturalists travelled with him – Mears, Heller and Loring – as well as his son Kermit, aged 20.[108] Amongst other items, Roosevelt brought with him four tons of salt for preserving animal hides, a lucky rabbit's foot given to him by boxer John L Sullivan, an elephant rifle and the famous pigskin library – a collection of classics bound in pig leather and transported in a single reinforced trunk.

The expedition began in Kenya and then continued through Uganda into the Belgian Congo and on by way of the Nile to Khartoum. The itinerary was carefully planned well in advance and Roosevelt wrote to his fellow American, Northrup McMillan, asking him for his help and advice. In the Library of Congress there is a letter amongst the Roosevelt papers dated August 19th 1908, which begins:

---

108 Kermit Roosevelt (1889-1943) was Theodore's third and favourite son. He shared his father's love of the outdoors, but was also an intellectual and a gifted writer. He was afflicted by spells of moodiness and eventually committed suicide.

My dear Mr MacMillan, I knew your uncle, the Senator very well and therefore I take the liberty of writing to you. People who come from East Africa disagree about many points, but they are all a unit in saying that you are the very best man to help the wandering hunter that there is out there and can do more for him than anyone else.

McMillan's reply to 'My Dear President Rooseveldt,'(sic) dated 29th September 1908, includes these words:

I hope you may find it convenient to come and stay with me, but whether or not it suits you to do so, I shall be delighted and make it a point to be here and to place at your disposal all information I have and also to place at your disposal any part of my staff of 15 Somalis, Shikaris, Syces, Mess boys, Cook etc, most of whom have been with me from five to seven years on my Blue Nile and Sobat expeditions and than whom I really believe there are no more capable men in Africa.

One does not need to go far afield from Juja to get practically everything in the way of game the East African plateaus afford. Most of the time vast herds of antelope of every description are to be seen in the Juja compound…Crocodiles and hippo are abundant in the Rueru at the foot of our garden and in the bush along its banks a mile or two below us, giant apes are plenty. Just hereabouts lion are comparatively abundant but difficult to get on account of hard ground making trekking nearly impossible…

Roosevelt also wrote to Frederick Selous and E N Buxton asking for their help and advice. One letter addressed to McMillan, but sent via Selous, mentions having lunch with Sir John and Northrup's cousin Amy, now Lady Harrington, and finding out about hunting conditions in Southern Sudan and along the Nile.

The presidential party sailed from New York to Naples, where they met up with Selous and then transhipped for Mombasa arriving in April 1909. At Mombasa Roosevelt was met by Frederick Jackson, the deputy Governor of Kenya, and the professional hunter R J Cunninghame, who was to act as his chief guide for his safaris in Kenya. Jackson entertained

Northrup and Lucie McMillan sitting on the steps of Juja House with Teddy Roosevelt (standing at right). Kermit Roosevelt is standing on the left next to Northrup.

Roosevelt and members of his party at the Mombasa Club[109] and then escorted them by train to Nairobi. Roosevelt particularly enjoyed his ride on the cowcatcher on the front of the engine.

As a result of this safari Roosevelt and his companions killed or trapped more than 11,397 animals from insects and moles to hippopotamuses and elephants. Between them they shot 512 beasts, of which there were 17 lion, 11 elephant, 20 rhino, and 262 animals were eaten during the expedition.

Tons of salted animals and their skins were shipped to Washington. The quantity was so large that it took years to mount them all and the Smithsonian was able to share many duplicate animals with other museums. Although the safari was ostensibly conducted in the name of science, it was as much a political and social event as it was a hunting excursion. Roosevelt interacted with renowned professional hunters and landowning families and made contact with native peoples and local leaders. On his return he wrote down his experiences in his book *African Trails - An Account of the African Wanderings of an American*

---

109 Roosevelt's reception in Mombasa proved controversial, as the banquet held at the Mombasa Club in his honour excluded non-members and boycotted the local press. Afterwards there were complaints in the newspapers that the important visitor had been monopolised by a certain clique.

Hunter. This was published in 1910 with 200 illustrations and quickly became a best seller.

Roosevelt's 1909 safari was probably the largest safari ever to be organised. It needed 500 porters, dressed in neat blue jerseys with boots slung round their necks, carrying everything from collapsible baths to cases of champagne. Newspaper reporters followed the steady progress of the ex-US president and the interest generated by such a high profile visit gave free publicity to Kenya and boosted its image considerably. Kenya came out of obscurity and became a desirable tourist destination.

In his book Roosevelt described his tent, his outfit and staff, and gave some idea of the logistical nightmare organising a safari on this scale must have been. The elaborate equipment and staffing and strict protocol had a distinctly Victorian feel, which later safaris abandoned in favour of more casual arrangements. His tent had a fly to protect from heat and a rear extension in which he bathed. There was a ground canvas to protect him from ticks, jiggers and scorpions and a cot to sleep on so as to be raised from the ground. For his personal use, he had two tent boys, one to look after his belongings and one to wait at table, two gunbearers and two horseboys or syces.

Out on safari Roosevelt wore boots and khaki trousers with knees faced with leather and the legs buttoning tight from the knee to below the ankle to avoid the need for leggings. He wore a sun helmet; reluctantly as he would have preferred his slouch felt hat, and a khaki coloured army shirt, with a pocket on the left but none on the right lest it catch the toe of his rifle stock. He had three rifles: a Springfield 300 calibre; a Winchester 405; and a double barrelled 500-450 Holland, the famous elephant gun. He carried field glasses and a telescope and a special scale for weighing game. In his pockets he carried a knife, a compass and a waterproof matchbox, as well as his gold mounted rabbit's foot for luck.

The US flag was borne in front of the column when the porters were on the move and when in camp the flag was planted in front of his tent. There is an illustration in his book showing rows of tents like a

Lucie McMillan with her pet cheetah at Juja.

military encampment, the porters at the back, the provision tents in between, and the officers at the front.

Roosevelt was interested to meet with the South African settlers as he himself was of Dutch descent. He rode on horseback through the plains and often shot from horseback, but he was not a particularly good shot as his eyesight was poor.

Chapter V of *African Trails* is entitled 'At Juja Farm.' During Roosevelt's seven-month visit to Kenya, he stayed on various settlers' land where he enjoyed the shooting and the hospitality.

"At Juja Farm," he says, "we were welcomed with the most generous hospitality by my fellow countryman and his wife Mr and Mrs W N McMillan." He stayed at Juja for one week and he praised the accommodation saying everything was "so comfortable that it was hard to realise we were far in the interior of Africa."

> Our hostess was herself a good rider and good shot, and had killed her lion; and both our host and a friend who was staying with him, Mr Bulpett, were not merely mighty hunters who had bagged every important variety of large and dangerous game, but were also explorers of note, whose travels had materially helped in widening the area of our knowledge of what was once the dark continent.
>
> Many birds sang in the garden, bulbuls, thrushes and warblers; and from the narrow fringe of dense woodland along the edges of the rivers other birds called loudly, some with harsh, some with musical voices. Here for the first time we saw the honey

guide, the bird that insists upon leading any man it sees to honey, so that he may rob the hive and give it a share.

Game came right around the house. Hartebeests, wildebeests and zebras grazed in sight on the open plain. The hippopotami that lived close by in the river came out at night into the garden. A couple of years before a rhino had come down into the same garden in broad daylight, and quite wantonly attacked one of the Kikuyu labourers tossing him and breaking his thigh. It had then passed by the house where it saw an ox cart, which it immediately attacked and upset, cannoning off after its charge and passing up through the span of oxen, breaking all the yokes but fortunately not killing an animal. Then it met one of the men of the house on horseback, immediately assailed him and was killed for its pains.

Later Roosevelt wrote about the menagerie he saw at Juja Farm and how many animals were kept in cages there: a leopard; five lions; and three nearly full-grown cheetahs. Lucy exercised the cheetahs on leashes and treated them as pets. Roosevelt noted they had non-retractable claws. There was also a tame warthog and a young gazelle looked after by a Maasai boy.

The stables at Juja with horses and their syces.

Roosevelt described at length in the Juja chapter one hunting incident featuring Northrup. Northrup went out hunting on foot with the young Kermit Roosevelt and a native beater, who surprised a leopard in the undergrowth, which charged straight at Kermit. Kermit had the presence of mind to shoot, but only wounded it. It ran in another direction and Northrup, standing on a termite mound, shot at it twice, but failed to kill it outright. The leopard turned on the beater in its anguish, seizing him with teeth and claws, until finally it died of the gunshot wounds. This leopard turned out to be a small elderly female, but nevertheless an extremely determined one. The trophy was sent back to camp with the injured beater and Roosevelt included a photograph in his account showing the hunter Bill Judd[110] putting permanganate[111] on the cuts suffered by the beater. The photo had the caption: "Taken by Northrup McMillan." Fortunately the beater was not seriously hurt.

Later on Roosevelt shot a rhino on the farm and Northrup sent out an ox wagon to bring it back to the house. An enormous beast, the rhino weighed just over 2,200 pounds. It was skinned and sent back as a trophy to the American Natural History Museum in New York.

One other incident involving the McMillans, which did not get a mention in Roosevelt's *African Trails* was the affair of the Ismaili lions. For their stay in Kenya, Northrup had lent the Roosevelts his town house in Nairobi, a spacious bungalow situated just behind the Norfolk Hotel in Parklands. Here, when he was not out hunting or visiting, Roosevelt would write and catch up on his business

---

110 Bill Judd, a Boer war veteran, first came to Kenya in 1902 as an elephant hunter. Northrup McMillan employed him as his personal hunter and paid him a handsome retainer to take himself and his guests out on hunting expeditions, whenever required. This proved so lucrative that Judd decided to go into business on his own. He owned a farm at Kabete. Over 6 feet tall and massively built, he was so strong it was said he could carry a mule on his back. He was one of the hunters chosen to accompany Roosevelt on his safari. Judd died in 1927 in a hunting accident.
111 Disinfectant crystals of potassium permanganate and a pair of small tweezers for extracting thorns were standard equipment carried by hunters on safari.

Northrup kept a pet lion at Juja House.

correspondence and Kermit[112] would enjoy nights out on the town with other young men. One evening, after a particularly riotous party at the Norfolk, on their way back past the newly built Ismaili mosque, the revellers removed the two stone lions that stood on the gateposts and brought them back to the house and placed them on either side of the fireplace. The stone lions remained there unnoticed for several days. The Ismaili community were understandably annoyed by the disappearance of their lions and they reported the theft to the police, and the missing stone lions were reported in the local newspaper. The lions were eventually discovered by, it is alleged, a visiting official who had come to pay his respects to Roosevelt. To preserve the Roosevelt good name and prevent any political fall-out with the Muslim community, Northrup was advised to quietly remove the lions and bury them on his estate. Northrup did this and the case of the missing lions was never solved and eventually forgotten.

However, it was not quite the end of the affair. In 1937, when Juja belonged to the Nettlefold family, the lions resurfaced once more. They were dug up when some thorn trees were being removed. To begin with it was assumed they were West African stone idols, representing

112 Kermit Roosevelt had a reputation for enjoying a drink and in later life became an alcoholic.

Ju and Ja, after which Juja had been named[113] - a seemingly obvious and satisfactory conclusion, to which members of the Nettlefold family still subscribe. But on further investigation by the Museum in Nairobi, the facts emerged. They were Indian lions, not West African gods. They made the connection and the mystery of the stolen stone lions from the Ismaili mosque was finally solved.[114]

As a result of the African Safari, Roosevelt became good friends with Mac, his special name for Northrup. There are more that twenty letters between them surviving amongst the Roosevelt papers in the Library of Congress.

Ex-president Roosevelt was not the only high profile American visitor to Juja. Edgar Beecher Bronson[115] a daredevil adventurer, hunter, writer and photographer, had stayed with Northrup a few months previously and sailed from Mombasa just as Roosevelt arrived, leaving behind for his ex-president all his guides and equipment. He dedicated his account of his African adventures entitled *In Closed Territory* to "that staunchest friend and steadiest shot, William Northrup McMillan." It was published 1910 with 100 photographs and was another bestseller.

A few months after the departure of the Roosevelt party, Carl Akeley, the famous American taxidermist, who had travelled out with Roosevelt, arrived to work on the specimens destined for the museums.[116] He camped on a site at Juja reserved for visiting safaris and stayed for

113 There is controversy as to the origin of the name Juja. Major Ringer may have suggested the name, as it certainly has a West African ring to it, in order to differentiate it from his farm, Long Juju. The headed notepaper for Juja originally showed two facing images – a monkey and an African head, with an ostrich in between, but this was changed to two heads. All kinds of superstitions were later woven about the imaginary idols and the name.
114 Cynthia Salvadori, *We Came in Dhows Vol III* (1996),106, "The Theft of the Khoja's Idols" by J Carver. This includes a picture of one of the lions.
115 Edgar Beecher Bronson (1856-1917) led an adventure-packed life as a Nebraska rancher, and West Texas cattleman. He had spent his youth in New Mexico, like Northrup, and they had many interests in common. Later in life he became a journalist on The Tribune and a writer.
116 Carl Akeley (1864-1926) pioneered the use of dioramas in museums and was also a naturalist and sculptor of note.

some time and got to know Northrup well. He later wrote how the farm abounded in game and was a popular place for shooting lion, which were very numerous in the area. On one occasion, he claimed to have seen 16 lions emerge from a cave on the estate.[117] Carl Akeley also recalled how Northrup, who had a pet lioness, which he kept by day chained to an iron ring embedded in cement near the front door, liked to watch his lioness in heat, in rut with a wild male, chuckling with delight as he sat in his chair safely behind locked doors.[118]

In the early days lions were often hunted with beaters. Thirty or forty porters would encircle the area of bush where the lion had been spotted and attempt to flush out the animal into open ground. When the lion ran out of its cover, the hunters on foot or on horseback rushed forward and gave chase hoping to shoot the frightened and bewildered animal dead with their rifles. It was a dangerous method and not infrequently the lion stood its ground and turned on its attackers. Hunters and beaters were often mauled and even killed. More scientific hunters like Carl Akeley, preferred the method of building camouflaged hides from where he could then lure the animal and observe it in its natural habitat before shooting it. This was a less exciting but safer way of hunting lion.

Northrup McMillan (right) with the hunter R J Cunninghame checking safari supplies for Prince Wilhem of Sweden. Northrup entertained Prince William and his travelling companion Count Gustav Lewen-haupt at Juja in March 1914.

There are many tales of how lions were specially lined up for important men visiting Kenya, so they could shoot their lion and take the trophy

---

117 Carl Akeley, *Brightest Africa* (1923), 159.
118 Penelope Bowdry-Sanders, *Carl Akeley: Africa's collector, Africa's Saviour (1991), 116.*

Winston Churchill stuck in the mud at Athi in 1907.

home as a memento of their visit.

Churchill, who visited East Africa in 1907 and went hunting at Athi but did not manage to shoot a lion, famously wrote in his book entitled *My African Journey* (1908): "Nothing causes the East African colonist more genuine concern, than his guest should not have been provided with a lion. He feels some deep reproach is laid upon his hospitality and the reputation of his adopted country." It is often claimed that Winston Churchill stayed at Juja, but I have found no evidence for it. Well-known visitors who did stay at Juja included Prince Wilhelm of Sweden, the Belgian Prince de Chimay, Rider Haggard, Lord Lonsdale, Sir William Dewar, Paul Rainey the hunter and Mr and Mrs Percy C Madeira from Philadelphia, besides a host of others.

One unusual visitor was the American Buffalo Jones who came with his group of cowboys. Northrup wanted to introduce the use of the lasso on his farm and he invited Buffalo Jones with his cowboys to Juja to try out their lassoing skills on the big game of Africa. There is a description of him sitting

Northrup McMillan with his pet warthog.

in a rickshaw in Nairobi watching them as they rode through town. Their dash ride through town whirling their lassos over their heads was an exact copy of the displays of Buffalo Bill and his troupe and must have been quite a spectacle for the residents of Nairobi.

> They (Americans) undoubtedly were great showmen, in fact they were great big boys. No gloomy creases disfigured their brows – everything was play. We few residents wore a smirk as we watched them walk along the street. What they lacked in stability of foot they made up for when they did a dash ride through town and with perfect timing and smoothness lassoed Northrup MacMillan as he sat in his rickshaw admiring the show.[119]

They brought over their cowponies and roped everything, even the larger species of game, but the experiment was not a success and did not catch on. Of the animals they tried lassoing the hartebeest was found to be the most dangerous and one of these gored and killed a cowpony.[120]

Northrup went on two hunting expeditions with Selous, starting from Juja. Their relationship was like that of a professor with a favourite pupil. Selous was the most sought after of all the professional hunter guides, but unlike others, he did not charge a fee, as it was all done on a gentlemanlike basis. Selous was content to enjoy his sport 'all found' while tutoring a wealthy novice, provided, always, that he was a congenial companion. He was fastidious about the company he kept and the opportunity to go hunting with Selous, the foremost and most famous expert on African wildlife, was only given to a chosen few.

Their first trip was in 1909 when for two months they hunted together in the Rift Valley, Thomson's Falls and Lake Baringo. Selous failed to shoot the black-maned lion he wanted, but as always with Selous, there was plenty of excitement. Northrup stopped a charging lion with a shot through the eye and another member of the party was

119 H K Binks, *African Rainbow* (1950), 103-4.
120 Errol Trzebinski, *Kenya Pioneers*, 139.

severely mauled. Selous returned to England in July. He had refused the invitation to join the Roosevelt safari as he said he felt uncomfortable in such a large crowd, but a more likely reason was that he disapproved of the planned orgy of butchery.

Selous agreed to go hunting again with Northrup in the spring of 1912, starting in January. This time they took Judd with them and visited the Uaso Nyiro River in central Kenya, now part of the Samburu Game Reserve, and the Lorien Swamp looking for elephant. Here Selous had an exhilarating horseback ride after giraffe and was badly ripped by thorn bushes. Northrup was horrified when he saw his hero come back covered in blood, but Selous was elated and bright-eyed saying happily that it had been just like old times.[121]

In a Christmas letter to Roosevelt, dated 22nd December 1912, Northrup gave a further account of his hunting excursion with Selous and described how he killed a lion he saw while riding back to camp after a morning shoot.

> He took refuge in a bunch of bush about a quarter of an acre in extent. The ground was good tracking ground, and I knew it had not left this bush as there was no spoor out of it. I crawled in on a rhino track some little distance and was lucky enough to see him lying down facing me and one shot from the 350 magnum through the head did the trick. I foreswore lions and thick bush some years ago, but must have been feeling particularly careless this day, and although it was very simple, I think it is a 'Mug's' game.

In Roosevelt's reply to this letter he advised Northrup not to do anymore 'bush crawling' after lion.

The high point for Selous was an encounter with an old buffalo on 25th March 1912, which he wrote up in an article for *The Field* magazine entitled 'My Last Buffalo.' Selous shot and wounded the buffalo, which he followed into thick bush and as he came up the side of a gully he heard the animal grunt and knew it was charging.

121 Stephen Taylor, *The Mighty Nimrod: A life of Frederick Courteney Selous* (1989), 275-6.

"I had not heard the sound for 20 years but once heard it can never be forgotten. The next instance he was on us with his nose outstretched, half a ton of bone and muscle driven at tremendous speed by the very excusable rage of a brave and determined animal. When I fired, the muzzle of my gun must have been within three yards of the buffalo. The animal fell but was so close that it struck Elani, a bearer who had been transfixed by the charge, a tremendous blow on the side with a horn. Another bullet quenched the last sparks of life in this brave old bull, which died as a buffalo should, fierce and resentful to the last. Elani suffered four broken ribs."[122]

At Oxford in 1906 at the opening of an exhibition of trophies at the later Pitt Rivers Museum, Selous described what was to him the attraction of Big Game Hunting. "Big game hunting is the hardest work in the world but it is the attendant disappointments, the privations, the difficulties and the dangers that make it the greatest and grandest of all sports."

Even at this early date Selous was concerned about the indiscriminate killing of wild game and he finished his speech by urging hunters to shoot in a fair and sportsmanlike manner and take only three or four specimens of each species and leave the rest alone, so as not to be a destroyer of wildlife.

Here Roosevelt, the other great master of hunting narrative, sums up the attraction and beneficial aspects of hunting as a pastime. His views reflected those accepted at the time, but which certainly would not be deemed politically correct in this day and age!

"In hunting, the finding and killing of the game is after all but a part of the whole. The free, self reliant, adventurous life, with its rugged and stalwart democracy, the wild surroundings, the grand beauty of the scenery, the chance to study the ways and

---

122 "My Last Buffalo," *The Field*, 8 June 1912.

habits of woodland creatures – all these unite to give to the career of a wilderness hunter its peculiar charm. The chase is among the best of the national pastimes, it cultivates vigorous manliness for the lack of which in a nation, as in an individual, the possession of no other qualities can possibly atone."[123]

---

123 Theodore Roosevelt, *The Works of Theodore Roosevelt, Vol II, XXIX* (1927), 29.

CHAPTER VII

CHIROMO
THE LION'S DEN[124]

While Juja was Northrup's especial project, Chiromo was Lucie's favourite home. Chiromo, unlike Juja House, was an elegant, stylish building, architect-designed. When it was first built, it was considered the finest building in Nairobi, easily outshining the Commissioner's Residence and the Bishop's House.

Ewart Grogan had bought the land in 1904 and the house was

Chiromo House in the McMillan era.

124 Nairobi Africans called Chiromo shamba ya bwana simba 'the lion's den.'

Lucie McMillan playing with her dogs in the garden at Chiromo.

constructed by a London architect, G H Cresswell,[125] with a firm of local Indian contractors during 1905. Grogan intended it to be his family home in Nairobi and he wanted it to be the finest house money could buy. He named it Chiromo after the Nyasaland settlement at the junction of the Ruo and Shire Rivers through which he had passed on his Cape to Cairo trek and which he had considered a shining example of what a European settler community in Africa should be. He had great hopes that Nairobi would turn out to be a city of similarly high standards and intended Chiromo to provide a benchmark for others to follow.

Chiromo was built in gabled Cape Dutch Style with a broad bougainvillea-clad veranda looking out over Nairobi to the Ngong Hills and the Athi Plains. The front door was made from thick mahogany with a leaded window bearing the initials ESG. Special wooden beams were imported, and some still bear the stamp – Grogan, Mombasa. Inside stood a large entrance hall with Canadian pine flooring off which led the main reception rooms. In the grounds of the 75-acre estate was a guesthouse, a small hunting lodge and ample stabling for horses.

Gertrude Grogan arrived with her two small daughters in 1906 and busied herself laying out a beautiful garden to surround the house. Ornamental ponds and fountains were planned and all kinds of foreign plants and trees were imported to see if they would grow in the altitude and climate of Nairobi. She immersed herself in the social life of the colony. There were about 500 Europeans living in and near Nairobi by this time. Then tragedy struck. Barely a year later in 1907 Gertrude became gravely ill and depression set in. Her distraught husband took

125 George Henry Cresswell was appointed Assistant Superintendant of Public Works for the East African Protectorate in 1904 and Executive Engineer for the Fort Hall district in 1905.

her back to England to recover and did not return for three years. He decided it was too risky to bring up a young family in Africa and left them behind in England allowing them out to East Africa only for short visits.[126] For much of the remainder of his marriage, Grogan was an absentee husband, requiring only basic accommodation in Nairobi.

Grogan rented out Chiromo, his lovely house on The Hill, first to Lord and Lady Cranworth,[127] and then to Northrup and Lucie McMillan from 1910. Sir James Hayes Sadler, the new Commissioner for British East Africa, used the guesthouse for entertaining as it had more spacious sitting and dining areas than Government House. In 1915 Grogan, suffering from one of his periodic cash flow problems, reluctantly sold Chiromo to the McMillans. Northrup had already sold his Parklands bungalow to Denys Finch Hatton and Jack Pixley in 1913 for £4,000.[128]

Chiromo House still stands and now forms part of the University of Nairobi. The house and grounds were left to the Queen Elizabeth College (as it was then called) after Lucie's death. From 1964-83 Chiromo House was leased on a peppercorn rent to the British Institute in Eastern Africa, who used the front of the house as the library,

126 Gertrude's Garden, the first children's hospital in Nairobi, was built by Grogan to commemorate his wife and was opened in 1948. She died of a heart attack in 1943.

127 Bertie Francis Gurdon, second Baron Cranworth (1877-1964) was an impoverished peer, who came to Kenya in 1907 in search of profit, adventure and sport. He set himself up as a commercial entrepreneur, who at one time traded top hats and mouth organs for ivory in the Congo. He was also a part owner of a sisal estate at Makuyu, and founder of the White Rhino Hotel at Nyeri. After WWI he decided to return to England. He was the author of several books about Kenya, the most well known being: A Colony in the Making (1912) and Kenya Chronicles (1939). He was married to Vera Ridley. Some of their happiest years were spent at Chiromo.

128 Sara Wheeler, *Too Close to the Sun* (2006), 66. Jack Pixley and Finch Hatton, two old Etonian chums, came out to Kenya together in 1911 and went into business forming the company Finch Hatton and Pixley Ltd, which bought and sold land holdings and stores throughout Kenya. Pixley and Finch Hatton also owned the Parklands House and a farm in Naivasha and a number of other speculative operations. The friends' joint venture was dissolved when Jack Pixley was killed in France in 1918.

while the director and staff occupied the rooms behind. The rest of the compound was used by the University and gradually became more built up. Nowadays the compound known as Chiromo Campus is completely filled with University buildings and only a small part of the garden immediately surrounding the old house remains. Enough

Chiromo House in the University of Nairobi campus in 2011.

remains, however, to give an idea of its former grandeur and elegance.

On the roof of Chiromo are placed two statuettes of a cat and a dog facing each other. The back of the cat is arched the tail held aloft in crooked alarm, ready to resist the approach of the jolly dog, who barks and wags his tail. Perhaps this is meant to symbolise the basic differences in nature of man and women or perhaps it is a subtle comment on the characters of the house's new owners: Lucie and Northrup.[129]

Lucie and Northrup were an odd couple; the man large and fat, the woman slim and elegant. It seemed to be a clear case of the attraction of opposites or the less charitable might suspect that Lucie had taken the practical decision, at the age of 27, to marry for money, not love. Their main common interest seemed to be a shared love of animals and nature. She was an expert horsewoman and in the early days a huntress of note. At Chiromo she kept a large stable of racehorses, with which she won many prizes and was keenly involved in the competitive world of horse racing and training. Racing appears to have been more her hobby than his. Northrup was content just to enjoy the spectacle and hand out the cups, many of which he sponsored. Lucie was refined and sophisticated, intelligent and resourceful, older than her husband. She was an energetic, adventurous, determined woman who liked to

---

129 The earliest photographs of the house do not show these animals on the roof, and so they presumably date to the time of the McMillans. I have been unable to find out who sculpted them or when they were put there.

travel and tended to overshadow her husband in company, being more than a match for her slow-witted and cumbersome husband. She was also a musician and an artist for whom an aesthetic and a cultural ambience was important. Like many of her social class, she was a snob and liked to mix with aristocrats and know all the right people.

Northrup, on the other hand, had little interest in the arts or high society. He was quite content as long as there was plenty of food and drink and friends around, with whom to have a good laugh. He loved wide-open spaces, the thrill of the chase and the fireside stories afterwards. He was kind-hearted, sociable and generous and enjoyed the pleasure of giving. He also liked to impress with his lavish spending. He had a rather childish nature, was not particularly intelligent and his ambitious projects inevitably met with failure.

Charles Bulpett, the perpetual houseguest, made up the third party in this strange ménage-á-trois. He had more in common with Lucie, with whom he seems to have conducted an Edwardian style, romantic friendship, consisting of flirtatious remarks and compliments and amusing conversation, but probably nothing more. But he was also close to Northrup, who relied on him for arranging his safaris and enjoyed his cheerful company. He kept a watchful eye on the McMillan properties in Nairobi during their frequent absences, a useful and trusted house sitter. After Northrup's death, Bulpett continued to live with Lucie at Chiromo. An acknowledged 'confirmed bachelor,' he was a charming, well-mannered and clever man with no money of his own. There is evidence that when he first met Northrup, he was heavily in debt and he borrowed £10,000 from Northrup.[130] A comfortable life in a millionaire household as a live-in friend, must have seemed preferable to a life of loneliness and penury in England.

Louise Decker, Lucie's personal maid, also lived at Chiromo and remained with Lucie until her death. Lucie had a very close relationship with Louise, who was like a mother to her and had been her nurse since childhood. Louise was a devoted and stalwart companion.Chiromo was the venue for many dinner parties and entertainments given by the McMillans.

130 Letter, 15 December 1906, Bixby papers in the Missouri History Museum Research Library, This letter mentions a £10,000 loan to Bulpett.

Here a poem dated 6th March 1913 and signed mysteriously by EKL and FVD extols the hospitality enjoyed there:

"McMillan's Bungalow"

There's a villa in Nairobi Town
Of great repute and great renown
Where lives a host of Juja fame
and where the guests drink much champagne[131]

Where Beauty, Fame and Wisdom meet,
And Music, Song and Twinkling Feet,
For this house has verandahs wide
And rows of chairs set side by side

Around the joyous festive Board,
Are seated Peasant, Statesman, Lord
And all with one loud voice acclaim,
'This house will live in Mem'ry's Name!'

The sick the sad, the anxious mind
Will comfort consolation find
The Traveller, Hunter, come from miles,
Lame Dogs are lifted over stiles.

There was nothing Northrup enjoyed more than involvement in happy occasions and his attendance of at least two weddings is reported in the local Nairobi newspaper *The Leader* for 1908. In October he gave a pair of silver candlesticks to Muriel Montgomery, daughter of Colonel Montgomery, Commissioner of Lands, on the occasion of her marriage to Ronald Carey, pleader at the court of Nairobi. Earlier in the year he gave the rather less magnificent present of a worked tea tray to Lucy Coldham of Ngoleni Fruit Farm on her marriage to George

131 Northrup always gave his guests a bottle of champagne each at his dinner parties.

The wedding of Violet Donkin to Donald Sharpe at Chiromo in 1917. Centre back can be seen the white haired Charles Bulpett. Northrup is standing on the far right and Lucie is seated third from the right.

Longridge. One of the bridesmaids was Miss Doris Lucas of Donyo Sabuk.

In 1911 Northrup financed the building of the YMCA in Nairobi[132] and later gave money towards the Scott Sanatorium, a settlers' convalescent home at Kijabe on the outskirts of Nairobi.[133] This was opened 7th June, 1913, by the Hon Mr and Mrs CC Bowring standing in for the Commissioner. Each patient paid seven rupees a night for a pleasant room and veranda. In the dining room was a large photo of Northrup McMillan, the chief benefactor. A private clinic, for Europeans only, it was run by Miss Denholme, with Miss Bateman,

132 This would have been for Europeans guests only and the intention was to provide low cost accommodation in a safe Christian environment in Nairobi for settlers and their families when they first arrived.

133 Named after Sir Henry Harold Scott, (1874-1956) an eminent physician who specialised in tropical diseases and hygiene. Whilst serving in the Boer War, he was the first to isolate the diphtheria bacillus and to identify veldt sores as an infection of the skin. He also introduced improvements in the treatment for tuberculosis and amoebic dysentery.

a trained surgical nurse and physiotherapist who was apparently 'well up,' in electrical treatments. It was doubtless a great benefit to the settler community. During WWI, when Violet Donkin[134] worked there, it was given over to the army and was used as a facility specifically to deal with dysentery, which was endemic amongst the troops.

Northrup at this period was a familiar large figure about town, often seen travelling in his buckboard drawn by four white Abyssinian mules. The driver of this distinctive means of transport was a Cape Coloured South African called Michael. He was ably assisted by a small Kikuyu, who crouched at his feet, dressed in blanket, ear ornaments and all the fixings, armed with a long lashed whip. At any given moment he would hop out, run forward to whip the off-leading mule, and then hop back on again, all with the most extraordinary agility. He likewise hurled what sounded like very opprobrious epithets at anyone who did not get out the way quickly enough to suit him. The expression on his face, which was of a person steeped in woe, never changed. The mules could travel at considerable speed with Northrup lounging in the back and rattled about Nairobi and down the Fort Hall Road toward Juja scattering all before him.[135]

Northrup had fingers in a number of financial pies and dabbled in various business ventures including coffee and rubber plantations. Generous and soft hearted to a fault, he could never resist a hard luck story and would help any European who appeared 'down and out.' Several of his 'lame ducks' were given employment on his estates, while others received loans or investment capital.

For instance he helped finance Major Ringer, who built the Norfolk Hotel, in Nairobi.[136] Major Ringer's Long Juju Farm had been anything but a money-spinner, but when Northrup purchased his land, Major Ringer was able to cut his losses, go in with a partner and start afresh

134 Violet Donkin was to have married Fritz Schindler, but he was killed by lion. She eventually married Donald Sharpe and was married at Chiromo in 1917 and the wedding reception was held at Chiromo - see photo.
135 Edward Stewart White, *Land of Footprints* (1913), 376-7.
136 The Norfolk Hotel still exists and remains one of the most famous and historic venues in town.

McMillan in his buckboard pulled by white Abyssinian mules in front of Juja House.

with a business more suited to his talents. With Northrup's backing, the Norfolk Hotel proved an immediate success. Hunting safaris would often start from the Norfolk and whenever Northrup was in town he would visit the bar and buy drinks for all and sundry. Robert Foran, a police officer, described how Northrup always attracted a large crowd of hangers-on, who were known as Juja ticks after the ticks that infested his Juja farm[137] When it first opened, the Norfolk Hotel was a long low building with hitching posts outside for horses, but it quickly became the most popular watering hole in town and expanded to meet demand. The bar at the Norfolk was always open and crowded, and it became a general meeting place for Europeans in Nairobi. It provided a fertile hunting ground for business agents waiting for opportunities to sell investments and land and fleece unwary newcomers and rich tourists.

There is the example of the Muthaiga Club, founded in 1912. This was financed by the fabulously wealthy and extremely generous Major Archie Morrison, who when visiting on safari was introduced at the Norfolk Hotel to a business agent called Freddie Ward,[138] who persuaded him to invest thousands of pounds in new business start

137 W Robert Foran, *A Cuckoo in Kenya* (1936).
138 Freddie Ward, born 1880 came to East Africa in 1903. He had a successful Estate Agent's business in Nairobi and later was an elected member of Legislative Council for Nairobi North.

ups. The story goes that Morrison insisted that his investments were conditional on there being a 'proper' club in Nairobi. To finance it he wrote out a cheque for £60,000 to Ward saying he would return to monitor progress, but never visited the Protectorate again.

This had a happy outcome and when the Muthaiga Club opened it had the best cellar in Africa, a shop that sold imported chocolates and other unheard of luxuries and a head chef, poached from the Bombay Yacht Club. On July 14th, 1914, there was a grand fancy dress party for the opening night. Uncle Bulpett was on the steering committee, Lucie McMillan gave advice on the interior décor and a proper architect, Tate Smith, had designed a fine Club House complete with classical portico. Northrup was one of the founder members and an enthusiastic patron of the dining room and bar facilities. Always large, this cannot have helped his waistline, which swelled dramatically as he approached middle age reaching the gargantuan dimensions of 64 inches. Muthaiga was built as a Settlers Club, to rival the Nairobi Club, which was patronised by government officials. It remains today the most prestigious club in Nairobi.

Less happy was the outcome for Bror Blixen, who was persuaded to swap the 700-acre dairy farm already purchased with his wife's family money for a larger coffee plantation at Ngong. He had come out in 1913 ahead of his wife, Karen Blixen, and had quickly found himself at home with the hard drinking, hunting set. Convinced by his new friends that coffee was the new gold, he unwisely bought the Swedo-Coffee Company from Sjogren, the outgoing Swedish Consul, who was returning to Sweden. This consisted of large acreages near Nairobi at Ngong and in Eldoret, in which Northrup also had an interest. The altitude seemed right, but what they did not know was that the soil was too acidic and there was not enough rainfall to grow coffee successfully. That deal, hastily concluded, was the seed of Karen Blixen's tragedy in Africa. She joined her husband in British East Africa early in 1914 and travelled out with Prince Wilhelm of Sweden who was visiting East Africa to go on a safari.[139] Northrup sent

139 Prince Wilhelm of Sweden stayed at Juja – a reference letter for a bearer, dated 10 March 1914 on Juja headed notepaper still exists and is proof of his visit. Jane Carver showed me the letter.

his cook for the train journey up to Nairobi and Denys Finch Hatton put the Parklands bungalow he had just bought from Northrup at the disposal of the royal party. The new Baroness Blixen experienced her first taste of colonial high society and was invited to dinner at Government House. Later she was to become a friend of the McMillans, but not until after WWI.

Jos Grant, the charming and easy going father of Elspeth Huxley, when he came out in 1912 fell into the clutches of Jim Elkington,[140] unscrupulous land speculator and master of the Masara Hunt, who was hoping to offload some of the 10,000 acres he owned at Chania Bridge, Thika. When the Grants arrived at the Norfolk Hotel, Elkington was at the bar and he and Jos immediately recognised each other as former schoolmates from the same house at Eton. Soon after there appeared on the scene Cecil Dashwood, a coffee planter from Kiambu and sometime surveyor, who offered to vet the land. The Grants ended buying 500 acres at £4.00 an acre from Elkington. Their new farm was three miles from the Kikuyu reserve and lay between the Thika and Chania rivers and needed complete clearing before any crops could grow. Here they built their house called Kitimuru and farmed with little success. The pains and pleasures of their early settling days was immortalised in Elspeth Huxley's famous book *The Flame Trees of Thika*.

Jim Elkington at Masara and the Grant's at Kitimuru, were a short ride from Juja. The Blue Posts Hotel at Chania Bridge where the Thika settlers would meet and drink was also close by. Everyone knew everyone and this was how farms were bought and sold and business was done in the early days. Informal dealings over a few drinks at the bar, a word in the right ear at a social occasion, this was the kind of closed, masculine world that Northrup understood and enjoyed. Add to this a dose of politics and Northrup was in his element.

After the death of Sir Donald Stewart, the next Commissioner of

---

140 Jim Elkington's estate was called Masara, where the stables were better built than the living quarters. Here, he kept his sixty foxhounds for Sunday meets. He was a keen horse breeder and importer of thoroughbred dogs and an occasional coffee farmer. He sold off half his coffee farm to the Grants, which helped his bank balance and kept him in drink for a few more years.

Kenya was Sir James Hayes Sadler, transferred from Uganda. He remained for three years and was known as 'Old Flannelfoot' due to his complete inability to make any sort of decision. Relations between officials and settlers deteriorated during his tenure as administration atrophied to an alarming degree and development of the new colony stagnated. It was with relief that Percy Girouard was welcomed as his successor in 1909. Girouard was a dapper monocled French Canadian engineer who had joined the British army in 1888 and had a formidable reputation as an expert on railways. He had reorganised the Egyptian railways for Kitchener and gone on to run the South African Railways for Lord Milner. He was no slouch and immediately took British East Africa in hand. Red tape was cut so as not to stifle enterprise, and over-mighty government officials were kept on a tight rein. He built the branch railway line to Thika and encouraged farming production and industry. He forged a better working relationship between officials and settlers and the economy improved by leaps and bounds. The Colonist Association and their conference meetings, called the Convention of Associations, under the leadership of Grogan, was given a voice in the policy making of the colony.[141]

By 1911 the country had begun to pay its way and looked a promising proposition for would be settlers. New settlers started coming. But in 1912 Girouard was forced to resign. The Colonial Office suspected he was too pro-settler and had dangerous separatist views. He was accused of moving the Maasai to make way for settler farms and had no option but to tender his resignation. His replacement was a more conformist colonial servant. Sir Henry Conway Belfield was a former barrister with no African experience to taint him or strong views to give officialdom cause for alarm. However, the boom years continued and the future of British East Africa that 'happy hunting ground of those, whose heart,

---

141 At this stage the Legislative Council, the body responsible for making the laws of the country, was still entirely made up of government officials and had no settler representation on it. This was a major bone of contention for the settlers who set up their own organisations. The Farmers and Planters Association founded in 1905 became the Colonists Association and in 1910 the Convention of Associations had its first meeting. Northrup is listed as vice-chairman of the Colonist's Association in 1909.

The Convention of Associations, which met in Nairobi in July 1913. Northrup McMillan is the tallest man standing in the centre at the back, framed by the archway. Lord Cranworth is seated in the centre at the front flanked by Lord Delamere (left) and Tommy Wood (right). Russell Bowker is the man with the large moustache second from the left end of the front row.

ideas and ambitions outrun the balance at the bank'[142] after an uncertain start, was set fair.

Early settlers have often been divided into three categories- Aristocrats, South Africans, and eccentrics.

The aristocrats came with money looking for opportunities to invest. They came in search of profit, sport and adventure, and a serious amount of cash was needed in those early days to build up farms and businesses from scratch. There was no get rich quick route; farming, the favoured enterprise in the early days, was a slow costly business, which did not show quick returns, indeed was more likely to turn in a loss. However, their experiments and failures opened the way for others to follow. These were men who were willing to take a gamble on an outside runner, spend their own money in risky ventures, to introduce new crops, livestock and

142 A favourite description of Kenya coined by Grogan. Edward Paice, *Lost Lion of Empire* (2001), 247.

farming methods in hitherto untried territory and by their enthusiasm encourage further investment and settlement.

South Africans were another important strata of settlement, who brought skills rather than money into the country. Mostly rough and ready frontiersmen, who understood the hardships of a pioneering life, they also came to farm, but on a smaller scale. Besides working their own farmsteads, they often provided the very necessary expertise and professional farming services for the larger farms of the aristocrat group. They were carpenters, storemen, carters, dairymen, etc. Initially many South Africans worked for Northrup on his farm at Juja. They played an essential part in the development of his estate, but their role diminished as the years went by, and their work was gradually taken over by Indian and African labour.

Eccentrics formed the last category of settlement and East Africa always had its fair share of misfits, madmen and dreamers, but the familiar figure of the profligate 'Remittance Man' did not make an appearance until after this period.

William Northrup McMillan, the American Big Game Hunter, Gentleman Buccaneer and Philanthropist with money to burn, did not quite fit into any of the above three categories.

He was a one-off, but nevertheless a prominent member of the early pioneering group, whose input was so important in shaping the future of Kenya.

CHAPTER VIII

A FASHIONABLE EDWARDIAN LIFE STYLE

Northrup was a restless man, a 'hot foot,' who never stayed anywhere for long. Besides his house and estates in Africa, he had a house in Mayfair, a rented country house in Devon[143] and returned each year to St Louis to see his mother at the family home in Portland Place. His world straddled three continents – America, Europe and Africa – and he was wealthy enough to live in all three. Whether or not he could properly qualify as a Kenyan settler is debatable as he rarely stayed in the country for more than six months at a time. In later life he described himself as a 'planter.' There was a distinction in the two terms; a 'settler' was someone who made the country their permanent home, while a 'planter' was one who lived there on a temporary basis, but retained a foot elsewhere.

Northrup was a dedicated Anglophile, who preferred the life in England to that in USA. As a wealthy American, he had an immediate entrée into British upper class society. He liked England as it was more cosmopolitan and less restrictive than America, where in each state a small inner clique of families ruled supreme – the Boston 400 were very snooty as were the southern aristocratic families of plantation owners.

---

143 This was Bicton, Lord Clinton's seat at East Budleigh.

Americans had their own class system based on old families. Northrup McMillan's name appeared in the social register of St Louis after 1903, but nevertheless Northrup was considered a nouveau riche and his Texan accent was not posh. He made much play on his old American middle name – Northrup – which connected him to the Mayflower pioneer settlers, but it was not enough to give him the ultimate social cachet he and, more particularly, Lucie wanted. On the other hand in Europe and in England, most people had no idea of the hierarchy and pecking order of American society, so Northrup could cut a dash and be accepted far more easily. In Britain to be Anglo-American was to be fashionable. Several impoverished aristocrats had married American heiresses, daughters of successful businessmen, who were now part of the ruling elite. Open-handed American millionaires were welcomed, with no questions asked about their antecedents. Money talked in Edwardian Britain, and successful industrialists were admired.

Life was great fun in Edwardian Britain for the upper classes. They enjoyed their sport and were extraordinarily good at arranging sporting events. There were the races at Ascot, Epsom and Cheltenham, where gentlemen in morning coats and silk top hats bet heavily on the horses and ladies wore hats and carried parasols in case of sun or more likely rain. There was rowing at Henley, yachting at Cowes, grouse shooting in Scotland and after that a spell in the South of France at Cannes or Nice at the casinos and perhaps a week in Baden Baden afterwards to take the cure and recover from copious intake of food and drink and heavy gambling losses. There was theatre going, music hall entertainment, grand balls and country-house weekends with fox hunting, and cards in the evening and discreet goings-on between the sheets, if your tastes ran in that direction.

The importance of correct attire for each event was stressed. Ladies wore special gowns with long sleeves for breakfast and a lady could only attend a play in black or dark blue, but evening dress and diamonds were de rigueur for the opera. When Lucie was presented at court she wore the regulation white ostrich feathers, pearls and a white dress with a long train.

There was a continuous round of pleasure to keep boredom at bay, designed for those who had no work to do and plenty of money to splash. A calendar of special events had been put together by Edward VII when Prince of Wales and in the years from 1900-1914 had become formalised into a rigid list of social occasions, squeezed into the British summer months, May - September, and known as 'The Season.' This was when mothers brought their eligible daughters to London to find a suitable husband. There was a great gathering together of fashionable society and a concentration of entertainments.

Only a select few could afford such a lifestyle, but those who could formed an elite group, known as the 'upper 10,000,' who all knew each other, or were of 'nodding acquaintance.' The chummy atmosphere was like belonging to a gentleman's club or being back at boarding school with its set rules and patterns of behaviour. It gave its members a sense of security in knowing where they stood and who they were. Edwardian society was characterised by strict codes of conduct and class distinctions, rituals and emphasis on dress and protocol. Form was favoured over content, charm and manners were prized above intelligence, while any claim to studiousness or serious thought could be a positive drawback to social success. It was the age of the 'English Gentleman' and the upper class twit with receding chin and sawdust between the ears, so memorably lampooned by PG Wodehouse.

It was Lucie who was the driving force behind the fashionable life they led. She had ambitions as a society hostess, while Northrup played the part of generous host. He was naturally gregarious and good humoured and with his height and impressive build immediately stood out from the crowd. He typified the British idea of all that was American, where everything including the country was fashioned on a larger and more expansive scale.

In the winter months, when English weather was cold and miserable, those who could afford it travelled to warmer climes. There had been great improvements in transport and the wealthy travelled more and further afield. Trains and passenger steamers provided comfortable and increasingly swift transport between continents and across oceans.

Luxurious trains such as the Orient Express, started in 1883, went to Marseilles and Nice in the South of France. The design of these trains was based on the American Transcontinental Railway, which had big passenger cars built as saloons and comfortable sleeping arrangements, hitherto unknown on European railways. The railway carriages were decked out with mirrors, carved woodwork and ingenious methods of turning upholstered seats into sleeping bunks for night travel. As a result of these improvements, the South of France became an increasingly fashionable destination.

It had become possible to cross the Atlantic Ocean from New York to Liverpool in less than a week. Super fast steamers, known as 'Ocean Greyhounds,' were fitted out with comfortable cabins, deluxe restaurants and bars. Deck games, such as quoits and shuffleboard, were organised on board to amuse passengers and in the evening they played bridge and whist and attended dinner dances. The McMillans' names turned up in several passenger lists as they criss-crossed the Atlantic. In 1898 Northrup was listed as a passenger on the Cunard liner *SS Cymria*, sailing from New York to Liverpool and he sailed again on the same ship in 1907. He arrived in Liverpool in May 1910 and in Boston, May 1913. Cunard and the White Star liners and Hamburg America and North German Lloyd ships all sailed the transatlantic route with ever more frequency.

Life on the ocean wave could be a liberating experience and a social leveller. Newly wealthy Americans barred from their nation's most exclusive circles could rub elbows with royalty and aristocratic luminaries and thumb their noses at those who snubbed them back at home. A transatlantic society was born where lines were blurred between nationalities forming a social group based on wealth rather than country of origin. The McMillans, who were constant travellers, belonged to this early jet-setting cosmopolitan group.

Special clothes were needed for transatlantic steamship travel. One list of essential attire for women included: one tailor-made suit; one pair of thick silk or woollen stockings; four sets of combination undergarments; a shirt waist; a sweater; a woollen wrapper for going to the bath; a dressy bodice for dinner; a pair of shoes with rubber soles; and three pairs of pyjamas. Men were required to wear a black coat for dinner, with stiff collar and tie. The bane of shipboard life was sea sickness for which there was no cure, but there was always a helpful steward to make sure your steamer chair was placed in a choice area on the deck, and to offer a word of advice on how best to find your sea legs.

To get to East Africa, Naples was the favourite port for transhipment. It was possible to get there by train or ship from Dover and was easily accessible from continental Europe. From Naples to Mombasa took approximately 19 days. The route went via Egypt, then through the Suez Canal, past Aden, Jibuti and down the Somali Coast. For first class passengers it was a pleasant experience and shipboard romances were not uncommon. Newcomers introduced themselves to Old Africa hands and acquaintances were renewed and useful contacts formed. Ewart Grogan met Sir Charles Eliot at Naples looking at the Aquarium, probably checking for sea slugs, which were his passion. Karen Blixen enjoyed a flirtation with the German general Von Lettow-Vorbeck in 1913 on her passage out to Mombasa. She was most impressed by his courteous manners. Roosevelt in 1909 met up at Naples with the hunter Frederick Selous, who had helped to organise his safari. Passenger ships from the German East Africa lines, the French, Messagerie Maritime, as well as British India Steamships, P & O and South African lines all sailed the route.

October was the month to visit Naples, when Russian and British royalty rented private villas along the Amalfi Coast and came to enjoy the balmy climate of Southern Italy. This was the time when the resort of Sorrento, made fashionable by the Astors, attracted the wealthy jet set, particularly Americans. They came to admire the beautiful bay of Naples with Vesuvius dominating the landscape, with its rosy peak forever changing colour and with occasional wisps of smoke puffing into the perfect blue of the sky above.

Passenger ships moored next to the impressive fortress on the waterfront at Naples. Conveniently close to the docks stood the grand opera house where performances of local tarantella dances and classical music could be enjoyed. A little further on up the hill the Archaeological Museum housed the extraordinary collection of marbles acquired by the Farnese Popes from the Roman baths of Caraculla. Restored with new arms and legs, these huge white statues provided an impressive vision of Roman antiquity. Perhaps even more interesting to Northrup would have been the secret collections of erotica from the brothels of Pompei. These were opened up for special visitors – gentlemen only – by special arrangement – dollars always assisted.

Lucie the culture vulture would have visited the sites of Pompei and Herculaneum and marvelled at the extent of the ruins uncovered from beneath the volcanic ash and mud. They would have sailed round the rocky Amalfi coast, reputed to be the most picturesque in Europe, with its steep inclines and charming views round each sharp bend. At Amalfi the little black and white striped church, perched atop steep steps, was dedicated to St Andrew, patron saint of Scotland – of especial interest for Northrup. St Andrew's body was interred in the crypt. Lucie with her painter's eye would have found it a paradise, with flowers and white washed buildings silhouetted against a vivid blue sea and little winding streets with open-air restaurants and bars and fishing boats pulled up on to the beach; the atmosphere marvellously soft and relaxing with mist and cloud dispelled by brilliant sunshine. Northrup would have enjoyed the fishing, and the seafood cuisine.

Horse drawn carriages took travellers up the steep slopes to luxury hotels with a view across the bay and the next morning to the small ferry, which went across to the fabled island of Capri. There was always time for an Italian holiday before boarding the ship for East Africa.

In London, Lucy redecorated the house in Berkeley Square[144] and rearranged the trophy room, which was overflowing with heads and skins and exotica from all their hunting trips. She was interviewed by the *Mayfair Supplement,* which described her as a prominent Anglo-American hostess.

144 19 Hill Street was an impressive four-storey Georgian terrace house, just off Berkeley Square. It had 10 bedrooms and a ballroom. It still exists today.

She spoke about of her exotic travels, her journey by mule across Ethiopia, her hunting experiences, and her narrow escape, when a lion sprang out of the bush quite unexpectedly. She had not faltered at this test of her nerve. In an instant her gun was at her shoulder, and a moment later the animal lay dead near her feet. A picture shows her posed, delicately coiffed and elegantly dressed, upon a settee in her boudoir, surrounded by French furniture, delicate rose brocade drapes and paintings of desert landscapes. She disclosed that she enjoyed the outdoor life and natural world above all else.

The McMillans as wealthy members of the Anglo-American Society were expected to help introduce American girls into British society, with an eye to an aristocratic alliance. Here is a description of a lavish dance they gave in July 1910 for the daughter of one of their St Louis friends.

Mrs William Northrup McMillan was another hostess of last night, when she gave a delightful dance, followed by a cotillion at her lovely house, 19, Hill Street. The floral decorations were beautiful, the ballroom being decorated with shaded roses arranged in large gold baskets, while an archway of roses was arranged between the two ballrooms. The staircase was decorated in a most novel way with carnations, while masses of the same flowers were used in the large marble hall. The dance was given for Miss Edwine Thornburgh, of St Louis USA, who looked lovely in a frock of pale blue chiffon over white satin trimmed with pale pink roses. The guests included Viscountess Falkland, the Earl and Countess of Ronaldshay, Countess Pappenheim, Lord and Lady Vivian…(long list of titled names). The presents were beautiful and came from Paris, while quite unique were the bangles given to the ladies, made out of the hairs of an elephant mounted in gold.

Miss Thornburgh was eventually successful in her quest for a husband. Two years later she married Sir Wilfred Peek, who she met at a Zoo party given by the McMillans at their house in 1912. The *St Louis Post-Dispatch* ran a prominent article on the society page entitled 'Miss Edwine Thornburgh to wed English Baronet,' which included a list of all the St Louis women, who had acquired European titles by marriage.[145]

A selection of Northrup and Lucie's hunting trophies went on display in 1910 in the British Pavilion at the International Shooting and Field Sports Exhibition in Vienna. An article describing the exhibits and the exhibitors appeared in *Country Life*. It was apparently the finest ever display brought under one roof and consisted of over 300 heads of game. Selous gave a keynote speech about the need for conservation laws and shooting licenses. Lucie lent her lion from 19 Hill Street and a rare black leopard, which were much admired, while Northrup had his heads of impala and Grant's gazelle exhibited alongside those from Selous' collection.

In December 1912 Northrup invited his friend Selous to join a shooting party at Bicton, the fine Georgian country house he rented at Budleigh Salterton in Devon, and described him in a letter to their mutual friend Roosevelt as being as 'spry and cheerful as ever.' Northrup had already paid several visits to Selous' house in Surrey called Heatherside, where he had built an extension for his trophy room and museum containing his birds egg collection and hunting memorabilia. There was nothing Selous enjoyed more than to take appreciative visitors round and show them his prize specimens

The McMillans' Mayfair House at 19 Hill Street, London, in 2011.
It has ten bedrooms and
a ballroom on the first floor.

145 *St Louis Post-Dispatch*, 5 November 1912.

and Northrup, his most fervent admirer, was a welcome guest. One of his favourite exhibits was a bull Kudu, which had horns 45 inches long – for a time the longest known pair.

Tatler and the society newspapers followed the McMillans' movements across the watering holes of Europe. In August 1910 they were spotted at Dinard amongst a number of other fashionable names, enjoying the French Riviera. Paris, Nice and Cairo were other favourite haunts of the McMillans, where they stayed in luxurious hotels and shopped and dined at famous restaurants; seen and being seen amongst the glitterati of the era. One year they went to India as guests of the Maharaja of Cooch Behar and went on a tiger shoot. They travelled continuously, globe trotting around the world as if afraid of staying still.

Whenever Northrup arrived back in USA, he liked to stop a few days at the Waldorf Hotel in New York to catch up with friends and business interests. Then he would often go to his mother's house in Magnolia, Massachusetts, which he preferred to the family home in St Louis, particularly in the summertime when St Louis was unpleasantly hot and humid.

One September day in 1911, while back on a short visit, he had lunch with Roosevelt at Oyster Bay. A scribbled note in McMillan's handwriting (one of the very few) on Waldorf Astoria headed notepaper survives in the Congress Library amongst the Roosevelt papers. It reads:

Dear Col. Roosevelt. We will be pleased to turn up on Thursday the 14th at one o'clock. We will motor down. The Juju major and my brother Henry Adams will also come with great pleasure. Very sincerely yours W N McMillan.

The Juju Major was Major CH Ringer owner of the Norfolk Hotel, while 'my brother Henry Adams' was Arthur Henry Adams, an American friend of the McMillans married to one of Northrup's cousins. Adams worked for the US Rubber Company and lived in

Paris.[146] There are several more friendly letters addressed to 'Mac' in the Roosevelt papers urging him to visit whenever he was in USA, but this is the only time McMillan appears to have done so.

On other occasions Northrup went deep-sea fishing in California. He was a member of the prestigious Tuna Club of Avalon, Santa Catalina Island, famous for its leaping tuna. He took part in fishing tournaments and won prizes for the enormous fishes he caught. He was a member of a number of exclusive clubs, namely: the Union League, Manhattan, New York; St James's Ranelagh Club in London; the St Louis Club; and the Noonday Club of St Louis.

In his hometown St Louis, Northrup donated some of his surplus trophies to the Zoo and, together with his mother, gifted a building at 3817 Olive St. for a Science Museum. The building was to house the headquarters of the Society of Scientific Research in St Louis as well as a free public museum, with collections of butterflies, Native Indian relics and botanical specimens.

The St Louis Daily Globe for December 20th 1911 ran an article entitled 'St Louis' greatest hunter of Big Game.' Later he is described by the same paper as a 'St Louis Aladdin in the heart of Africa's wilds living like a Nabob on his 20,000 acre ranch.'

The Edwardian age is sometimes imagined as a romantic golden age of long summer afternoons and garden parties; a perception created by those who looked back with nostalgia across the abyss of war. But historians generally consider it as a mediocre period of pleasure between the great achievements of the Victorian period and the catastrophe of World War I.

---

146 Arthur Henry Adams (1869-1915) tragically died on the Lusitania. He was married to Gertrude and had a son William McMillan Adams, who was educated at Eton.

CHAPTER IX

THE WAR YEARS AND A KNIGHTHOOD

World War I (WWI) was a watershed moment in history, when the old order was swept away and society was changed forever. It was also a time when Northrup stepped up to the mark, when his most admirable qualities came to the fore and he offered help when it was most needed. His generosity and steadfast support during wartime earned him grateful friends and admirers in all walks of life. The success that he had failed to find as explorer, farmer or businessman, now came to him in the least expected field of endeavour.

Like a domino effect, when a seemingly trivial malfunction sets off an explosion further down the line, WWI was set in motion by the assassination of Archduke Ferdinand in June 1914 in Sarajevo,[147] the capital of Serbia. This cruel deed exacerbated old enmities between countries and as battle lines were drawn former diplomatic alliances and treaties came into play. Britain was drawn in when Germany threatened neutral Belgium and they entered the war as an ally of France in August 1914. Everyone was curiously eager for a fight. There had not been a proper European war since the Crimean War of the 1850s. Britain

---

147 He was heir apparent to the Hapsburg Austro-Hungarian Empire.

grandly announced that they were fighting for the 'Balance of Power.' Sir Edward Grey, the Foreign Secretary, looked out of the window at Downing Street and uttered his famous lines: "The lamps are going out all over Europe. We shall not see them lit again in our lifetime."

Sir Henry Belfield, the governor of British East Africa, did not want to go to war with neighbouring German East Africa. Relations had always been most cordial in the past and he saw no reason why quarrels in Europe should have to spread to Africa. British East Africa was totally unprepared for war. It had just 2,400 regular soldiers, consisting of the officers and askaris of three battalions of the King's African Rifles (KAR), available in the whole of British East Africa. Of these, one battalion was stationed in Uganda and one in Jubaland. But all hopes of avoiding conflict were dispelled when German forces invaded at points along the 500 mile border with German East Africa which ran from the coast inland to Taveta near Mount Kilimanjaro and up through Lake Victoria to Uganda. Volunteer soldiers rushed to defend their land, with varying success. The Germans took Taveta on 14th August, 1914, but the invasion in September, targeting the port of Mombasa, was held at Gazi, by the gallant Major Wavell and his Arabs – mostly water-carriers recruited from the Old Town, armed with ancient rifles and whatever weapons came to hand. They held the line until a company of the King's African Rifles came to their relief and drove the Germans back across the border. In Nairobi farmers mounted on horseback gathered at Nairobi House, headquarters of Grogan's business empire, and vowed to fight. They formed themselves into units, reminiscent of medieval Crusaders, with names such as 'Bowker's Horse,' 'Cole's Scouts,' or 'Monica's Own.'[148] Lord Delamere was one of the first to come forward and Freddy Ward was put in charge of recruitment. 1,200 men enrolled in total and were loosely incorporated under the banner heading of the East African Mounted Rifles. These volunteers provided a vital stopgap army until the arrival of regular soldiers from India, South Africa, Rhodesia and Britain.

Northrup was in America when war broke out. His mother Eliza

148 Named after the attractive daughter of Governor Belfield. She liked to watch the soldiers on parade and eventually married Freddy Ward.

had been suffering with a heart condition for a number of years, but her health had worsened suddenly and he and Lucie had gone to be beside her sick bed. In December, they moved her from St Louis, to Pasadena, California, hoping the warmer climate would bring relief, but to no avail and she died there on 15th January 1915. Her remains were brought back to St Louis and she was buried with her husband and two dead children in the family mausoleum at the Bellefontaine cemetery.[149]

On her death Eliza McMillan left nearly $5,000,000, an enormous sum of money for that time, but of this only the family home in Portland Place and $100,000 was left directly to her son and heir Northrup.[150] The chief executor of the will was Bixby. It was a complicated will, with many bequests and a large amount of money left in trust. The will was

The McMillan Mausoleum at Bellfontaine Cemetery, St Louis.

reported on extensively in all the local newspapers, as Eliza McMillan was one of the richest women living in St Louis. In addition to family members, to whom she left sums of money and property outright, she also left annuities to more than fifty others including friends and members of her household staff.[151] This later led to several lawsuits concerning the beneficiaries. Lucie was left the house in Magnolia, Massachusetts. Eliza had already made large donations for a Hospital at the University during her lifetime.[152] Now the residuary of her estate

149 The McMillan Mausoleum contains just four burials, the infants Mary and Percy who were transferred there in 1873, and William and Eliza.
150 Northrup immediately put the house up for sale and it was bought in 1915 by Jackson Johnson, president of a large shoe company.
151 Reports, *St Louis Daily Globe*, January 1915.
152 Washington University in St Louis, Department of Special collections, Olin Library, Building Files. The McMillan hospital became part of the modern medical complex called Barnes Jewish Hospital, and the medical school of Washington University.

was to be left in trust, with the proviso that if Northrup died childless, as seemed likely to be the case, all the money was to go to the McMillan Eye, Ear, Nose and Throat Hospital.[153]

At about this time Northrup made two passport applications in quick succession – one in October 1914, which was for a new passport and again in February 1915. In the first he called himself a capitalist, signed an oath of allegiance as an American Citizen, and also made the statement that he was domiciled in the United States, his permanent residence being St Louis. It further stated: "I am about to go abroad temporarily and intend to return to US within three months." In the second application, presumably because the three months had lapsed, he applied again for permission to travel, stating he was a commercial businessman and intended to go to England and France, no time frame given. Due to wartime conditions, overseas travel had become more restrictive and difficult. America had not yet joined the European war and American citizens were neutral bystanders.

The news from East Africa was not good. In November 1914 the expeditionary army sent from India had been soundly defeated by a far inferior force of Germans at the coastal port of Tanga. Despite an overwhelming ratio of 8 to 1, the British had been ignominiously beaten and had evacuated the troops, leaving huge amounts of supplies and ammunition on the beach for the Germans. Inland, things had not gone much better and the fighting north of Voi had stagnated, with the strategic town of Taveta still in German hands. *HMS Pegasus* had been sunk in Zanzibar harbour and the German battle cruiser *Koenigsberg* had eluded the British Navy and gone into hiding in the Rufiji Delta. The professional soldiers sent from India known as Indian Expeditionary forces 'B' & 'C' appeared not to have improved the position, but rather to have made it worse.

On 22nd November the War Office had assumed responsibility for the War in East Africa, but the rivalry and dislike between the Indian army and the colonial forces of the KAR made the task of creating

---

153 There is a handwritten letter addressed to Lucie offering to impregnate her so as to secure the inheritance, the writer's credentials being that he had already fathered six children. W N McMillan Scrapbooks RH, Micr.Afr. 641.

a workable British army in East Africa very difficult. When British regulars, Indian Army Units, Colonial volunteers and the KAR tried to work together, the initial result was frustration and confusion. There was a lull in the fighting during early 1915, but the ill feeling between soldiers and settlers persisted. Ewart Grogan tried to persuade the Governor to put the colony on a war footing, but Sir Henry Belfield refused to listen. In January 1915 Belfield declared the local defence force was no longer needed and many volunteers drifted back to their farms. The Governor remained resolutely anti-war and went deep-sea fishing off Mombasa, while his civil servants returned to their desks and customary duties.

In America Northrup read the news from East Africa with increasing dismay. He was anxious to leave America and get to England and learn the fate of his friends. With his mother barely cold in her coffin, he nevertheless decided to leave for England on the first ship he could find and join up.

In London friends of British East Africa came together and decided to send out a specialist force. It seemed the regular Indian army was proving disastrous at coping with conditions in Africa, while the colonial forces were few with poor leadership. Something had to be done! Colonel Daniell Patrick Driscoll,[154] 55 years old, who had served in the Upper Burma Rifles and had won a DSO leading Driscoll's Scouts in the Boer War, now called for volunteers to form his own 25th Battalion the Royal Fusiliers, otherwise known as the Legion of Frontiersmen, to serve in East Africa. He personally chose and vetted the 1,166 men he recruited. The age limit was 25-48 years old, but it was obvious that many of the old-timers must have forgotten the year in which they were born. The Legion was formed on 12th February 1915. Northrup applied and was accepted, but as only British subjects were eligible to join the British army, he had to sign naturalisation papers.[155]

---

154 Colonel Daniel Patrick Driscoll (1862-1934) settled in Ruiru after the war.
155 Undated article from St Louis Globe in W N McMillan Scrapbooks RH, Micr. Afr.641. "McMillan was in St Louis at the outbreak of war, but soon after his mother's death sailed for England, whence news came in May that he had become a British subject and joined the British army with the rank of Second Lieutenant."

He was eligible because of his Canadian parentage. Frederick Selous had also joined the Legion and somehow persuaded Driscoll to get him a commission despite being over 60 years of age. Northrup at 41 was within the age limit, but with a 64-inch sword belt, his enormous bulk and weak health made him poor fighting material; his expertise would have to be used elsewhere.

Known as the 'Old and Bold' or the 'Boozaliers,' the Legion of Frontiersmen consisted of an extraordinary mixture of adventurers from all walks of life. It had a definite flavour of Boy Scouts for adults. There were big game hunters, cowboys from Texas, several former members of the foreign legion, a footman from Buckingham Palace, a number of circus acrobats and clowns, seal poachers from the Arctic Circle and a Scottish lighthouse keeper. Other recruits were privates McCrae, who had been with Shackleton's polar expedition, and Synott, the ex-heavyweight boxing champion of Australia. There was also an ex-colonel of the Honduras army accompanied by his private bodyguard. They were undoubtedly brave men and few were to return. They left aboard the *SS Neuralia* from Plymouth on 10th April and arrived in Mombasa 4th May 1915. They were the only Battalion of the BEF (British Expeditionary Force) to embark and enter the field without prior training.[156]

The first major battle to involve the Frontiersmen was at Bukoba on Lake Victoria, in June, where they joined forces with soldiers of the Loyal North Lancashire Regiment. Here Northrup "fought for two days beneath equatorial sun and stormed crags and cliffs under fire of machine guns and rifles"[157] and was promoted from Second Lieutenant to Captain. At Kisumu a force of about 2,000 men, under the command of Brigadier General James M Stewart, were loaded aboard four old lake steamers and ferried across to the eastern end of the lake to the small German-held port of Bukoba. The original plan was to surprise the Germans at night, but the moon was too bright so the attack was postponed until the next morning. Instead the troops were landed at

156 The regiment was finally disbanded on 29 June, 1918.
157 Article headed "Rich St. Louisan Plucks Captaincy from Cannon's Mouth in East Africa," *St Louis Globe*, W N McMillan Scrapbooks RH, Micr.Afr.641.

the foot of a steep cliff three miles north of the town. To begin with a mutiny threatened as the regular soldiers refused to advance over such uninviting territory. After some protest they did, but it took them more than a day to cover the distance and many of the troops spent an uncomfortable night in the open without food or water. Fortunately as the Germans were not expecting an attack from that direction there was little resistance and the next morning they took Bukoba. They burned the German fort to the ground and dismantled the wireless communications. Very hungry and thirsty, the victors looted the town. It was not one of the more glorious episodes of the war, though this was glossed over in the reports sent to Europe and the US.[158]

In August the Frontiersmen were deployed at Maktau defending the line of the railway, which passed close to the border near Voi, but Northrup was not with them. He remained behind the lines and was employed in the Commissariat, the supplies section. Proud of his promotion, he had himself photographed in uniform with his captain's stripe, looking fat and nonchalant holding a cigarette in a long cigarette holder. Grogan heaped praise on Northrup for his actions during the war. He could have remained neutral, but he chose not to, and came to help his friends and share their hardships. It was the ultimate gift of friendship from a generous and courageous man.

On September 7th 1915 Northrup chaired the influential meeting called by Grogan at the Theatre Royal in Nairobi, to try and raise morale and instil more fighting spirit into the colony. The evening started with patriotic songs and music before Grogan rose to his feet amidst the cheers of the 1,500 present. He gave a landmark speech calling for conscription and exhorting the whole country to become involved and more pro-active in the war. In front of an emotive audience, he castigated the Governor and his officials for happily tending their gardens and playing tennis, while men at the front were dodging bullets. He criticised the public works department for doing nothing to help the soldiers. He did not have kind words for those settlers either, who had returned to their farms and washed their hands of the war leaving it all

158 Theodore Roosevelt congratulated his friend Selous on "a first class little fight at Bukoba."

to the regular soldiery. Everyone, he claimed, needed to be involved to bring the war to a swift and successful conclusion. He pointed to Northrup as an example of someone who was doing above and beyond his duty in helping to win the war. Northrup had offered Chiromo as well as his farm at Juja for use as a soldiers' convalescent home[159] and Grogan declared that he was ready to follow this magnificent example by offering his estate at Turi as a camp for women and children. His stirring speech was met with thunderous applause and members of the Indian community, who had not previously been notably supportive of the war, were moved to voice their support as well. Russell Bowker, plain speaking as ever, declared that it was indeed "time to shoot straight and stick together."

This meeting proved a turning point. Governor Belfield changed his tune and agreed to take on a more active role and involve all settlers in a joint war effort. He immediately summoned Grogan and Northrup for talks and one week later agreed to their demands for a War Council and conscription. The War Council was an immensely powerful body chaired by Charles Bowring[160] and empowered to rule the colony virtually by diktat. It met every morning and framed resolutions, which were then passed to the governor in the afternoon. A few days later a slip of paper would come back to the committee informing them of action taken by the Governor and within a few weeks many of the suggested measures had actually been enforced. In the first three months the Council passed resolutions at the rate of more than one

---

159 This was rather less generous than it sounded as it was only for officers of the Legion of Frontiersmen.

160 Charles Calvert Bowring (1872-1945) was an important colonial official, whose long-standing service and extensive knowledge of the workings of Kenya colony were essential for the success of the administration. He first arrived in Kenya in 1895 and was appointed to the Audit Department, becoming Treasurer in 1901. In 1911 he was made Chief Secretary of the Colony and in 1917-19 Acting Governor. Of similar age and interests to Northrup, he was a Fellow of the Zoological Society and of the Royal Geographical Society. His wife was well known for her tireless hospitality. It was hard working officials such as the Bow-rings, who provided the backbone for colonial government in Kenya and kept the country operating smoothly.

a day. Originally the War Council comprised of three officials, two soldiers and three unofficials - Grogan, Northrup McMillan and J J Toogood, the general manager of the Standard Bank.[161] One of the first things the council did was to require all European civilians – men and women – to register and then they were either sent to the front or designated essential jobs. As Elspeth Huxley points out, the War Council probably achieved more action in a short time than any other body in Kenya before or since.

British East Africa was now placed on a proper war footing and Northrup, the anglophile American, had become one of the de facto rulers of the colony. It was an extraordinary turn of events, which could not have been envisaged. Only in wartime could such a situation have developed.

An interesting letter written by Northrup survives amongst the Roosevelt papers in the Library of Congress. It is dated 1st February 1916, and describes the War Council work in more detail and his life in wartime Nairobi.[162]

> There has been a good deal of sickness in the Battalion, and my two hospitals which I opened at the beginning, (my town house and my farm), have been full up the whole time.

> Since July, when I was made Base Commandant of the Battalion, I have been in constant residence in Nairobi, and have only been out on flying weekend trips to Juja, inspecting patients and arrangements.

He goes on to describe the September mass meeting and the formation of the War Council, which "for some months sat for five days a week and ran this country."

---

161 Lord Delamere joined this body in 1917 and his chief contribution was to make sure the colony was fed in wartime. He kept the farms running and organised which basic crops were needed.
162 The letter is actually addressed to Edward Stewart White, who had visited Northrup at Juja in 1912.

The heavy work is now finished and we only need to meet once a week to handle small details that crop up from time to time. An outcome of this same mass meeting was the formation of the Woman's War Work League and they are doing most splendid work in providing substitutes in offices, shops and other places to free men for active service, making, sorting and supplying comforts and necessities for the troops, training nurses and cooks for the hospitals and other useful work. Miss Livingstone of my Chiromo home, has the class in cookery.

We also inaugurated a done day's pay donation per month for a fund called the 'Government House Fund,' which will take care of all cases of distress in this country after the war is over. Every person and soldier in the protectorate gives at least one day's pay per month to this fund, and it will amount to a good many thousands of pounds before war is over.

We also instituted a non-treating act, which has been of immense benefit especially in the towns. Before it was passed hospital patients without money would be allowed to go for walks in the town and country. After two or three hours they return to the Hospital more or less in a state of inebriation, entirely due to the misplaced generosity of friends and admirers. The non-treating act has put a stop to all of this.

We also passed a regulation that no men in uniform should be supplied with liquor, except at meals, before six pm. This was necessary as a precaution to the troops from overseas who did not realise what the tropical sun meant and disregarded the rule of no liquor being taken in the middle of the day. The large amount of fever and sunstroke that has existed here amongst the troops has been entirely due to alcohol in the daytime.

Another scheme that is being brought forward is that of giving a grant of land to every man fighting for the Protectorate. In this way we hope to settle up the country to a large extent and to settle a substantial force from South Africa and overseas in the newly acquired German territory...

We had quite a cheery time at Christmas, both here at Chiromo and at Juja. Major Grogan and I joined forces Christmas Eve, and gave a Christmas Tree (Party) at the Muthaiga Club to forty small children of our acquaintance. The children seemed to enjoy themselves tremendously, but I believe the parents and nurses who attended with them enjoyed it even more than the kiddies. There were five or six little ones who had never seen a Christmas Tree before and had never seen a Santa Claus and when Santa Claus appeared through the skylight in the roof and came down a ladder, these little ones were terrified and bolted for the blue with frantic mothers and nurses pursuing them. They were all pacified, however, eventually, and the evening went off pleasantly.

The next day being Christmas we had quite an elaborate Christmas dinner for the patients both at Chiromo and Juja. There were about thirty in each home. They had a real home Christmas dinner, including turkey, mince pies, plum pudding and ice cream. The men had an impromptu concert among themselves in the evening and the Medical Authorities allowed us to give them a bottle of beer each, and they had quite a cheery evening. We had our own dinner at night, which consisted of the Chiromo staff and fourteen other guests, so we sat down to table eighteen strong. We had invited as guests here all the unattached men and women amongst our friends that we could think of and nicknamed it the 'Lonely Ones Christmas Dinner.' We were all very merry, and I am afraid kept things up rather late.

I was very sorry that my wife and party had changed their sailing so that they did not arrive here until 18ᵗʰ January and missed all our Christmas festivities. They however arrived well and safe and we were all pleased to see them. Lucie, Miss Harvey,[163] Mr Bulpett and myself all live in little temporary cottages, which have been erected in Chiromo grounds. They are quite cool and comfortable and we take our meals with the rest of the staff in the Home. Lucie is starting nursing work, Miss Harvey is taking on the secretarial work of the show and Mr Bulpett is having a trial run as secretary of the local war relief fund.

The turn of the year between 1915 and 1916 saw a definite improvement in British fortunes in East Africa. Smuts, the experienced South African general, took overall command and slowly but surely drove the Germans back. General Von Lettow-Vorbeck, the wily German commander, began his famous fighting retreat drawing the British further and further into German territory, but at least the British were making headway albeit it was slow and tortuous.

Captain McMillan continued with his military duties with the 25th Royal Fusiliers.

In March 1916 he was made Post Commandant Mbarara, and on 8th August 1916 he was transferred to Post Staff Officer Mbuyuni, in charge of the camp there. Mbuyuni is a small hill in the shadow of Kilimanjaro about ten miles east of Taveta, which for some reason was chosen as a military base for the campaign in 1916 to retake Taveta and regain control of the border with Tanzania. Safeguarding the railway line was always a major concern as it provided a vital supply route for Kenya and Uganda.

More is learned about Northrup's contribution to the war from letters written by Theodore Roosevelt to Frederick Selous.[164] In one he says that he is glad that McMillan is doing well with the Commissariat and in another 'Roo' sends his warmest regards to Mac.

Selous returned briefly to England in June 1916 to be operated for piles, but was back again in East Africa by August having helped

---

163 Miss Jane Harvey was Northrup's personal secretary and on his death she was given an annuity, which was included in his will.

164 J G Millais, *Life of Frederick Courtenay Selous* (1918), 326-327.

recruit 400 new men for the Legion of Frontiersmen. He then went to Tanga waiting to rejoin The Frontiersmen, who were by this time deep in enemy territory, fighting inland from the Rufiji Delta in an area called Kissaki. In Tanga he lived in a house with Captain McMillan for eight weeks.[165] Northrup was there to oversee the deployment and provisioning of the reinforcements before they were sent into the field of battle. He persuaded Selous to give evening talks to the men to keep up morale during the waiting and Selous recounted his early adventures in South Africa and exciting hunting tales, which helped to alleviate the boredom and anxiety of the men. Though Selous was a shy man in company, he was an enthralling public speaker, who would bring his experiences vividly to life, almost acting the part.

In December Selous and his new recruits were entrained to Dar es Salaam and then to Mikessi. From there they walked for two weeks to meet up with the regiment at Kissaki. A few days later the 25th Battalion, the Royal Fusiliers, moved towards the Beho Beho Hills and there Selous was killed by an African sniper while leading his company in action on January 5th 1917.

Selous was buried near the camp, under a tamarind tree, a simple wooden cross marking the spot. Fittingly his burial place lies in the area of the Rufiji Delta, which has since been made a wild life sanctuary known as the Selous Game Reserve.

Northrup, still stationed in Tanga, was devastated by the news of his friend's death. Bulpett sent him a telegram of commiseration from Nairobi. "I cannot tell you how sorry and shocked I am by

Frederick Courteney Selous, DSO, was a Captain with the 25th Royal Fusiliers when he was killed by a sniper in German East Africa in 1917.

165 ibid, 346.

his death," while Lucie sent him a long sympathetic handwritten letter from Chiromo saying how desperately sad she was and how she longed to comfort him and put her arms around him as she knew how much he had loved and admired Selous.[166]

The two had become good friends. Northrup had learnt bush craft from Selous and also an increased respect for wildlife and its habitat. They had hunted together. Selous had stayed with McMillan, both at Juja and the house in Devon on a number of occasions and they had exhibited trophies jointly at the important Exhibition of 1910. Selous had progressed from hunting for sport and the thrill of the chase to becoming a renowned naturalist and collector, who only shot to add a perfect specimen to his collection or to increase the knowledge of a rare species. Northrup followed his mentor's lead and as he aged became a far more discerning and responsible hunter.

*Northrup McMillan
in military uniform, 1915*

A memorial bust of Selous was unveiled in the British Museum of Natural History in 1920 and in his memory a bronze buffalo, designed by H Clark, was placed in the main lounge of the Nairobi Club. This model was later adopted as the crest and badge of the Kenya Regiment. Northrup gave generously to the subscriptions for both these memorials. It was the least he could do for a man whom he had idolised for over twenty years.

A few months after the death of Selous, Grogan and Northrup were sent on a mission to collect abandoned enemy supplies along the

---

166 Letter and telegram in W N McMillan Scrapbooks RH, Micr.Afr.641.

Northrup McMillan (left) sitting in the back of an army truck smoking a cigarette with his friend Ewart Grogan standing beside him.

Tanga-Taveta railway. There is a photograph of Northrup sitting in the back of an army truck smoking a cigarette, while Grogan stands beside him. The border by now was fully in British hands and much of the German railway as well.

Grogan and Northrup worked well together during the war. Together with Lord Delamere, they had become the most powerful non-officials in the colony, running the country through their seats on the war council.

Grogan had the ideas and Northrup backed him up, providing money to put proposals into practise. It was a perfect combination. When Bowring considered disbanding the War Council and dispensing with the non-official representation in the Government, Grogan and Northrup countered by getting together with other investors and buying the East African Standard. In this way they controlled the local press and made sure settler views received maximum coverage to prevent officialdom gaining the upper hand. Governor Belfield was recalled to London in 1917 and there was a period of interregnum of 22 months before Governor Northey was appointed in January 1919. During this period Charles Bowring stood in for the Governor and Grogan and McMillan continued to have great influence in the affairs of the country, even after the war council was finally discontinued.

Both Chiromo and Juja were now in use as hospitals for the Frontiersmen and Lucie and Louise Decker were personally helping to roll the bandages, hand out tea and provide home comforts for the wounded heroes. Northrup, who could count on £70,000 a year,[167] a vast income for the time, paid the running costs.[168]

He did not forget the hardships suffered by the African troops, who had fought alongside the European soldiers, and a letter from the McMillan scrapbooks showed how he sent supplies and stores to the KAR Hospital for Natives from his estates. One personally signed list dated 30th July 1917, included 22 cases of limejuice, six cases of Ideal Milk and four of potted meat, some boxing gloves and about 100 emergency Medical Cases for Officers. It is on record that he liked to arrange boxing matches and displays to amuse the troops as well as other sporting entertainments.

Less affected by the economic downturn hitting Europe, Northrup was able to help his adopted country and old friends, who had fallen on hard times and his generosity did not go unrecognised.

In early 1918 he was promoted to major and recommended for a knighthood for 'unusual services' and, although an American, he accepted. The notice duly appeared in The London Gazette that Major McMillan was knighted by Letters Patent dated 6th February 1918. Later there was controversy about this acceptance of a British Knighthood, as American citizens do not usually accept knighthoods, or use the title 'Sir.' But Northrup became a substantive knight, only open to British subjects and made use of the title 'Sir,' as he had renounced his

---

167 Edward Paice, *Lost Lion of Empire* (2201), 272.
168 Letter from war office to GOC troops in East Africa Nairobi, dated 29th August 1915: "I am commanded by the Army Council to inform you that they have had brought to their notice that Lieut MacMillan, 25th Battalion Royal Fusiliers, has placed his two houses at the disposal of his Battalion as a convalescent home, and he is himself defraying the cost of upkeep."

Military top brass visit Chiromo when it was a convalescent home during World War I.

American citizenship at the beginning of the war and had now become British. He could do this because his parents William and Eliza were born in Canada, which was part of the British Empire, and did not become American citizens until 1874, two years after Northrup's birth. Technically, Northrup was born British.

This was not the first time an American citizen had forsworn his citizenship in order to accept a title. H M Stanley, the famous explorer, had done the same. He had refused a knighthood from Queen Victoria when he first came back from Africa, as he was not then eligible, having taken out American citizenship. But later he accepted one in 1899 after he was naturalized and became British once more.

Northrup was immensely proud of his title and so was Lucie. Titles meant a great deal in Kenya in the early days, as most of the prominent settlers belonged to the British aristocracy and many of the chief officials received knighthoods for services rendered. For the McMillans it meant recognition and position. They could now claim to be part of the establishment and high society in Kenya. In the McMillan scrapbooks more than fifty letters of congratulation were carefully stuck in and kept, filling up almost half of the second scrapbook. The letters and telegrams were from old friends, colleagues, those who had been helped by his generosity, parents of wounded soldiers cared for in his convalescent homes and ex-soldiers who had fought with him. All of them showing how popular and well-respected Northrup had become and Northrup lapped up their praise and flattery basking in the adulation.

CHAPTER X

PAINFUL POST-WAR ADJUSTMENTS

The outlook in British East Africa, which had seemed so promising before the war, received a serious set back due to the four years of conflict. Administration required a radical rethink, infrastructure desperately needed modernisation, and agriculture needed a complete overhaul. Years of hard work had been lost and the country was in dire need of new strategies to kick-start the economy again. Gone were the carefree, adventurous days of the early pioneers and British East Africa, soon to be renamed Kenya, was entering a more troubled phase.

Just a few weeks before the final surrender of the German army on 25th November 1918, Sir Northrup and Lady McMillan held a charity garden fete in the grounds of Chiromo House. Billed as the largest of its kind yet attempted, it aimed to raise money for a ward in the Star and Garter Military Hospital in Richmond, London. Many prominent names appeared in the newspaper write-up, doing their bit to raise funds for the care of severely injured soldiers. Mrs John Ainsworth ran the white elephant stall, Mrs Henry Boedeker acted as fortune-teller, while Mrs Leslie Tarlton supervised the refreshment tent. There were strolling clowns, a curio stall and a flower stall. Karen Blixen along

---

with other well-known settlers joined in this major social event, which was followed by a night of fun and frolic to the music of the KAR band.[169] The war was at last over but there were many burning issues in need of urgent attention and in the ensuing months and years there were to be few causes for celebration.

In January 1919 the new governor of British East Africa, the dapper Major General Sir Edward Northey, arrived, a monocled and autocratic herald of change. He was greeted by a long and belligerent speech given by Major Ewart Grogan, leader of the settler party. In the fog of war the settlers had taken the initiative and had acquired a say in the running of the country, and they had no intention of relinquishing these powers without a fight. They were wary of Colonial Officials, who they thought wished to return the country to the pre-war administrative position, when settlers had no recognised voice in government at all. Governor Northey listened and reassured them that an elected body, a Legislative Council with settler representation, would be set up along the lines of the British Parliament. The country was divided into 11 electoral areas, and two unofficials were offered seats on the inner cabinet, the Executive Council. Besides the eleven elected Europeans, there were seats allocated to one elected Arab member, two elected Indian members and a missionary to represent African interests. On the government side were ten ex-officio members and seven nominated officials representing government policy. This gave the government an automatic majority of at least two. The first elections were held in February 1920 and Sir Northrup, a former War Council member, was elected to Leg Co (as it was always subsequently known) as member for Ukamba District.

Governor Northey also acceded to one further suggestion from the War Council – the request for more European settlement. The soldier settler scheme was put into action in 1919. The country needed commercial activity and more land to be farmed and made productive and this idea seemed the perfect solution. 250 small farms and 800 large farms were made available. The small farms of 160 acres were handed out free, but the larger farms had to be paid for and all applicants had

169 W N McMillan Scrapbooks RH, Micr.Afr.641.

to be vetted for suitability and show a minimum income of £300 a year. The scheme proved popular and there were more than 2,000 applicants for the draw, which took place in June 1919. Two revolving drums were kept busy all day. A name was drawn, then a number, which showed the order in which the applicant could choose his farm from the list issued by the Government. In November 1919 a ship was laid on called the *Garth Castle*, which brought in more than 1000 new and hopeful settlers.[170] The farms were located in and around Nanyuki, Kericho, Kiu and TransNzoia, and most started with dairying and pig production, or maize and wheat crops. The majority of the settlers stayed to make a go of it, although the struggle to make ends meet was often severe. Many relied on bank overdrafts and loans to keep their farms going. In 1927 eight years after the scheme started, 770 of the 1031 farms allotted were still in possession of their original owners.[171]

More troublesome was the provision of labour in the colony, which came to a head at this time. The crisis over labour arose because the new settlers required manpower to help clear, plant and work their land effectively, but the native population was not so keen to provide it. The question then was asked: what kind of pressure should be brought to bear on native Africans to stimulate them to work? The argument went like this: as the soldier-settler scheme had been promoted by government, government had a duty to provide the new settlers with adequate labour for their farms. Previously, manpower had been provided on an ad hoc basis. The District Commissioner would talk to the local chiefs and they would round up some young men to do the required work. Big farmers like Delamere or Northrup McMillan would enter

170 About 4,736,000 acres had been alienated before 1919. This scheme added 2,888,000 acres more. This meant 12,212 square miles were set aside for white settlement out of a total land area of 240,000 square miles. Native reserves made up 48,345 square miles. Elspeth Huxley, *White Man's Country: Lord Delamere and the Making of Kenya Vol II* (second edition, 1953), 56.

171 One sad failure was the British East Africa disabled cooperative, which ran a farming community financed out of the pooled savings of their semi-crippled members. They bought 25,000 acres near Kericho – but gambled all on flax, which slumped badly. The members lost their savings, but had they experimented with tea instead, the story would have been different.

into private agreements of their own with local headmen or set aside land on their farms for squatters, who would then bring their families and livestock and live there rent free in return for six months labour in every year. In the early days, when food was scarce, labourers were often paid in maize and wheat, which was gratefully received. Amongst the Destro photographs dating to c 1905-1906 are pictures of Kikuyu women dancing in delight around a *kikapu*[172] of maize cobs, earned

African labourers waiting for their wages outside the store at Juja Farm.

Kikuyu women dancing for joy round the bag of maize, wages for working at Juja Farm.

in return for working at Juja Farm. There are also pictures of casual labourers outside the farm store at Juja waiting for their rations of corn.

Elspeth Huxley's parents used to put an oil lamp outside their house when they wanted help and simply wait for curious natives to turn up. This was all very well, when settlers were scarce, but now a more organised system was clearly needed.

The new labour laws were all tied in with the need for revenue, and the introduction of taxation and a wage economy. Unless Africans went out to work and were paid in money, money would not enter the reserves in any quantity and hut tax could not be collected. More

---

172 Swahili term for a basket.

money must be made to circulate before the Government could raise the larger revenue it so badly needed. Native ordinances were passed to regulate labour policy. Any African who left his reserves and entered employment now had to carry with him a certificate of identification – the dreaded *kipande* or identity card, which meant his every movement could now be tracked and he could not avoid his hut tax. Squatters on European farms now had to be paid a set wage for their labours. Sir Edward Northey in his opening speech to the first session of Leg Co in April 1920 spearheaded the push for Africans to join the labour market, when he said, "It is a duty to encourage the energies of all communities to produce from these rich lands the raw products and foodstuffs that the Empire requires."

Back in UK, the so-called native ordinances were criticised as harsh and draconian.[173] Missionaries gave sermons in pulpits about natives in Kenya being ruthlessly exploited and there were awkward questions asked in parliament about African tribesmen being forced to work under legal compulsion for the benefit of private individuals. But labour was needed in order to build the railways, provide public buildings and produce foodstuffs. However unpopular the measures were, the colonial government had to find ways of harnessing the available manpower so the country could forge ahead.

An even more painful adjustment was the 'Currency Crisis,' aptly named by some the 'Shilling Swindle.' This was triggered by the need for increased circulation of money. As part of the economic stimulation package, the colonial government decided to introduce a new currency for Kenya. The problems arose when the former unit of East African currency, the Indian rupee, was transformed into the new currency,

---

173 It was John Ainsworth (1864-1946), who was responsible for these new laws, which are often simply known as the Ainsworth Native Ordinances. John Ainsworth a former employee of the IBEACo came to Kenya in 1888 and worked first as a Transport Superintendant and then as a District Sub-Commissioner. During WWI he was made Military Labour Commissioner for the EA Expeditionary Forces and was put in charge of native army recruitment. Ainsworth was an exceptionally efficient and dedicated government official, but his precise and singleminded approach did not make him universally popular. In 1920 he retired and returned to the UK.

shillings. The colonial office, which now ran Kenya from London rather than from Bombay, wished to link the currency to the British pound rather than the Indian rupee, but there was great confusion about where to fix the exchange rate (stabilisation as it was called) at the point of changeover. Since 1905 the rate of exchange for rupees had remained fixed at 15 rupees to a sovereign, the gold equivalent of a British pound. This meant one rupee was worth one shilling and four pence and all transactions were based on this calculation. But after World War I, with the British economy in free fall, the currency was taken off the gold standard, which allowed the exchange rate between pounds and rupees to fluctuate according to the supply and demand of the markets and the two currencies were no longer linked together and to the price of gold. In the immediate post-war period the Indian rupee strengthened against the pound, almost doubling in value. After considerable debate the Treasury Department decided to 'stabilise' the new Kenyan currency at two Kenyan shillings to a rupee, and new coins known as Florins were minted to replace the old rupee. But no sooner had the decision been taken than the value of the rupee dropped and kept on falling until it was back to its original rate of one shilling and four pence. This was a disaster as the East African Florins, two shilling pieces replacing the old rupee, were now only worth one shilling and four pence on the open market. Businessmen and farmers lost a great deal of money. There were furious debates in Leg Co as all loans contracted by producers and bank overdrafts in sterling were increased literally overnight by almost 50%. Settlers who went to bed owing £5,000 woke up owing £7,500 and had to continue paying interest on a fictitious £2,500, never borrowed. There was a terrible furore.

Such was the uproar, Governor Northey suggested the exchange rate be adjusted back to the old rate and fixed at one shilling and four pence to the rupee, instead. However, when this proposal was taken to the Legislative Council, it was thrown out. On the evening before the special session, a meeting had been held between the bankers and elected members, when the bankers warned them that the proposed change would ruin the country's credit and mean it would be necessary to call in all overdrafts and foreclose on mortgages. Leg Co lost its nerve and capitulated and the shilling was introduced at the originally agreed rate of two shillings to the rupee.

Further difficult decisions were made in 1921, when wages were cut by 33% to compensate for the losses suffered by farmers and businesses, but such was the confusion over the exact value of the new shilling, this went relatively smoothly. One shilling coins were minted the same size as the old half rupee and most labourers when they received their wages did not realise they had been short changed and that the shilling they received was actually only three quarters the value of the old half-rupee coin. A pay cut had been affected by sleight of hand.

Northrup was a member of Leg Co during this turbulent period, and so was involved in the background of the policy making. He was never one to make speeches, but generally supported the settler line and voted with them. When looking through the reports of the third session of Leg Co, which sat in Nairobi, November 1920 – March 1921, his name hardly ever crops up, although he was in attendance.[174] He was however moved to speak on the Currency Crisis and raised concerns about the effect it would have on soldier's pensions. He spoke a few times on the alienation of crown lands and the soldier-settler scheme and in January 1921 he proposed a motion to appoint a committee to consider what amendments might be made to the existing mining laws of the colony. To begin with he was in favour of re-adjusting the rupee to the one shilling and four pence rate, but when on 29th March 1921 the final vote was taken on keeping the higher rate, we are told that "the Hon Sir Northrup McMillan signified his agreement with the proposals."

This first Kenyan Legislative Council with elected settler representatives has received bad press in later history. Members have been called spineless for meekly falling in with the government's wishes. Grogan had failed to get a seat on Leg Co and Lord Delamere, who by this time had taken on the mantle of leader of the settlers, was

174 Kenya Legislative Council Proceedings 1911-23, Rhodes House, ref 753.13s1.

scarcely ever in the country. He was doing battle on behalf of Kenyan settlers back in England. Tommy Wood, a Nairobi businessman who sat on the inner cabinet, was the next most senior settler, but he appears to have been lacklustre in leadership. One has a vision of the enormously fat Sir Northrup sleeping through the endless speeches and debates and occasionally grunting his approval, while the fabric of Kenya was transformed.

To add to the woes of this troubled period in Kenyan history, racial tensions began to raise their ugly heads. The so-called Indian Question, which was never satisfactorily resolved, and was to cast a blight on racial relations for many years, came to a head between the years 1920-1923. The seeds of trouble were sown immediately after the war, when the settlers were feeling in a particularly aggressive and confident mood. At the January 1919 meeting of the Convention of Associations (known as 'Grogan's Big Noise') a petition was sent to Governor Northey. This asked for a limit to be put on Indian immigration and requested that they should not be given a vote on the soon-to-be-reformed Legislative Council and should not be allowed to acquire land in the highlands, which was to be reserved for white settlers only. At this period the settler group lead by Grogan had high hopes that Kenya would become a primarily white dominion, like Australia or Canada, and ultimately become self-governing. They further claimed that Indians were a bad influence on Africans. The Indian population in Kenya understandably took great exception to this petition and in retaliation sent a deputation of their own to the Secretary of State for the Colonies, Lord Milner, in London, requesting equal representation and rejecting the principle of segregation.

The Indian population in Kenya was several times greater than the European population. Furthermore, particularly in the coastal regions, they had been settled for a good while longer than the Europeans. When the Europeans first arrived at the end of the 19th century it was the Indian traders who gave them invaluable assistance. When the railway was built, it was done with Indian expertise and labour. When the protectorate was first proclaimed it was linked to the India Office and the first administrators and their clerks came from British India. Even the legal system and land ordinances were based at first on Indian precedent. The currency in use was the Indian rupee. In the pre-war period relations had been harmonious and the Indian leaders presumed an equal partnership in the development of the colony.

The balance shifted after the war, when many more settlers came from Britain and responsibility for Kenya was taken up in London. The currency was linked to the British pound, rather than the Indian rupee, and colonial officials were increasingly sent straight out from London, with no experience of India. The formerly strong ties with India were cut.

Unlike the British settlers, the war had not affected the Indian population, who in some cases had prospered. Few had joined up to fight, unlike the Africans, and many had gone back to India only to return again once the discomfort and danger of war was over. They were carpenters and builders, skilled mechanics and traders. Many ran *dukas,* small shops along the railway line and in the native reserves. They tended to have a greater understanding and closer relationship with the Africans than the Europeans.

Indian demands for equal representation seriously alarmed the European settlers who could envisage a scenario of being squeezed out by the far more numerous Indians, who would then run Kenya as an extension of India. The Europeans resented the brown wedge driven between black and white in Kenya and did not want to share the colonial experience with Indians. They became extreme in their views, claiming that Indian radicals were politicising young Africans and were a source of

A M Jeevanjee on the steps of his house in Nairobi with General Smuts.

trouble in the colony. The success of Gandhi in mainland India sent shudders through the colonialists, who didn't want his politics to permeate through to Kenya.

Lord Delamere took the lead in representing the white settler view, while A M Jeevanjee, a prominent Indian Muslim businessmen, led the Indian side.[175]

Most Africans were persuaded to side with the Europeans claiming they did not want to be ruled by Indians, though Harry Thuku, secretary of the Young Kikuyu Association, created a temporary panic, when he sent a series of resolutions passed by his organisation and a telegram to London in support of the Indian viewpoint.[176]

New elections to Leg Co were held in 1921. Northrup retained his seat and this time Grogan was returned. The Indians rejected the miserable two seats they were allocated and agitation continued. Hopes in the Indian camp were rekindled when Churchill became Secretary of State for the Colonies. He had visited Kenya in 1907 when he attended a luncheon given by Jeevanjee and had seemed at that point to be pro-Indian and appreciative of Indian contributions to the colony. However, after the meeting of January 1922 the Indian delegates led by Jeevanjee were bitterly disappointed by his lack of support and the sentiments expressed in the pledges he gave. These were: 1. Highlands to be reserved for European settlement; 2. Equal rights for all civilised men; 3. Regulation of Indian immigration in the interest of the native population and British settlers. He also gave one more promise; Kenya in the fullness of time was to be self-governed.

---

175 Zarina Patel, *Challenge to Colonialism* (1997). The struggle of Alibhai Mulla Jeevanjee for Equal Rights in Kenya. This book, written by the grand daughter of A M Jeevanjee, follows in detail the tortuous twists and turns of the Indian Question and gives a view from the Indian side of the argument.

176 It was later claimed that he had been bribed. He had attended a party given by one of the Indian leaders, who had offered him money and a free trip to Europe in exchange for support. His telegram read: "Native mass meeting held Sunday 10th. Over two thousand natives present declared Indian presence not prejudicial Native advancement as alleged by Convention of Associations. Next to Missionaries Indians are our best friends." This viewpoint was promptly denied by the supreme chief of the Kikuyu, who lent his weight to the British camp.

In August 1922 Sir Edward Northey was suddenly recalled as he was considered too pro-settler in his views and Sir Robert Coryndon was sent down from Uganda to implement the Wood-Winterton Agreement, which was about to cause another perfect storm amongst the European settlers in the colony.

The Colonial Office, alarmed by growing civil unrest in India, had decided to give in to Indian demands in Kenya. The agreement

Lord Delamere, from a portrait presented to him by grateful settlers in 1923.

enfranchised all Indians, allowed unrestricted immigration and abolished segregation. The European settlers were furious and organised themselves into a Vigilance Committee, with plans to kidnap the Governor and take to the streets and fight if need be, rather than accept the implementation of the ruling. Governor Coryndon hesitated, unwilling to spark a confrontation. He expressed his reluctance to London to enforce a decision entirely in Indian favour. In 1923 another delegation went to Downing Street headed by Delamere to meet with the prime minister and express the settlers' serious discontent.[177] Indian representatives went as well to put forward their side of the argument. It was back to stalemate. Delamere argued that the Indians had no justification for demanding a say in the government. The Indians replied that if they couldn't have equal representation, then the Europeans had no right either to a voice in the government of Kenya and it should be left up to the officials. The arguments rumbled on throughout 1923. Finally, in a meeting of the British Cabinet the decision was reached

177 It seems that Northrup was part of this delegation, but he did not play any significant role other than making up numbers.

to refuse Indian demands for a common roll and leave settlers in possession of existing political rights. The British Government feared armed rebellion in Kenya. In July 1923 it was proposed that the Indian representation be increased to five seats and the colonists demands for a greater measure of self-government be turned down.

The 1923 Devonshire Declaration further stated that "Primarily Kenya is an African territory and HM Government thinks it necessary definitely to record their considered opinion that the interests of the African natives must be paramount, and that if and when those interests and the interests of the immigrant raccs should conflict the former should prevail."

Leg Co voted to accept the terms of the Devonshire Declaration – the best that could be hoped for out of a bad bargain – but the East African Indians denounced the settlement and called it a 'gross betrayal.' They refused to pay taxes or vote in the next election and did not fully participate until the elections of 1931. Fortunately for the stability of the colony, the East African Indian community was a diverse one, made up of many different religions and peoples, who did not all pull together, so the policy of civil disobedience was only taken up by relatively few cases.

The final outcome of the Indian Question was unsatisfactory on all sides and served only to deepen the divisions between the various communities, which continued up to Independence. The European settlers never forgave the East African Indians for spoiling their pitch. The Indians felt betrayed and undervalued. The Africans were caught between the two. Both Indians and Europeans now viewed the Colonial Office and its officials with deep mistrust, as their promises and pledges were so easily broken. It was a sad affair that had been badly mishandled.

It is difficult to know where Northrup stood in the matter of the Indian Question. He left no papers and as he rarely spoke in Leg Co his personal views went largely unrecorded. In the earlier period he had been a keen supporter of Grogan's politics, which had an Olympian, Rhodes-ian, view of Africa, with its dream of linking

East, Central and South Africa into a corridor of exclusive British power running the length and breadth of Africa, with interconnected trade and transport networks. But this grandiose vision of a British Imperial Africa had been superseded and was categorically denied in the 1923 Devonshire White Paper, with its new emphasis on temporary trusteeship and native interests being paramount. Grogan's style of politics was becoming increasingly old fashioned and no longer main stream and most settlers transferred their allegiance to Lord Delamere with his more limited goals of increased representation, controlled Indian immigration and everyone working hard for a prosperous Kenya. Northrup, who liked to think of himself as part of the establishment, had a natural propensity to side with the majority standpoint and the official view. When The Devonshire White Paper was voted through Leg Co, he sent the following short message to his Ukamba Constituents: "Congratulate Kenya on the Settlement of the Indian Question. Our constitutional principles have been endorsed. We should accept these with a good grace and get on with the business of the country."[178]

Northrup began to work more closely with Lord Delamere, who had reached the conclusion that the best way to stem the flood of Indian immigration and head off the possible Indian take-over bid, was to train up Africans to do jobs currently being done by Indians. In 1924 Northrup helped fund a training college for African artisans in Kabete. This college also aimed to give the students the experience of good food and lodgings to incline them towards living under better conditions when they left. He gave his support to a body called the European and African Trades Organisation, which enforced a boycott against Indian artisans and acted as an employment bureau to place skilled African workers. EATO also lent money to Africans who wanted to start up businesses in the native reserves and helped to set up native markets. Also in 1924, Northrup put money into a new teacher training college in Kabete, which was the first to be established in East Africa. The college was based on the American

---

178 Newspaper cutting in W N McMillan Scrapbooks RH, Micr.Afr.641.

experience of educating Negroes in the Southern States and not only trained African students to become teachers but also to become leaders in their rural communities.

Northrup was often away and unable to attend the business of Leg Co and Major J C H Grant stood in for him whenever he was abroad or absent.[179] In 1923 Northrup sat on a select committee to investigate the conditions in the Maasai reserve and the disturbances and in August 1924 he was appointed a provisional member of the Executive Council during the absence of Lord Delamere. Northrup's motto was 'quietly does it' as he was not at ease with the noisy quicksilver cut and thrust of the usual political stage. His thoughts came slowly and words did not flow easily off his tongue, so he preferred to stay in the background and play a supporting role. Nevertheless, his benign presence and steady support for the settler cause was undoubted and seems to have been enough to convince his constituents that he was representing their interests well.

The funds he gave to Delamere's African training initiatives were all done in the last year of his life, but it was an indication of the new direction of his political thinking and the way in which politics were changing in Kenya.

---

179 C S Nicholls, *Elspeth Huxley: a biography* (2002), 59-60. This was Jos Grant, Elspeth Huxley's father. He entered politics in 1921, but because of his absence during the war he was five days short of the two years residence required for Legislative Council candidates and Sir Northrup McMillan won the Ukamba seat. However, when McMillan left for a visit to the USA, he invited Jos to stand in for him, offering him his luxurious American car to use while he was away. Jos sat on the Currency Committee and on a commission to inquire into the conditions of labour.

CHAPTER XI

AT HOME AND ON SAFARI WITH THE MCMILLANS

We get a peep through the keyhole and a rare close up glimpse of the McMillans at home and at play from a diary kept by William Keeney Bixby. For two months in February and March 1921, Bixby wrote a day-by-day account of his stay with the McMillans and his safari experiences with them.[180]

Bixby had known Northrup since he was a boy in St Louis. This same Bixby had risen to become Northrup's father's trusted right hand man and chosen successor in the car foundry business. It was he who engineered the amalgamation of several smaller car foundries into the giant American Car and Foundry Company, hereafter known simply as ACF, with William McMillan as chairman of the Board and Bixby as managing director.

Bixby had retired early but remained on the board of several financing companies, including the St Louis Union Trust Company, in which Northrup had investments. He had looked after the family

---

180 Travel Diary 1921-22, W K Bixby Papers (WTU 00013) Washington University in St Louis, Unversity Library, Department of Special Collections, Manuscript Division.

finances since William McMillan's death in 1901 and was a shrewd financier, who kept the money flowing to fund Northrup's lavish life style. Bixby resided in Portland Place, St Louis, in a house in the same street as the McMillan's former family home. He lived in considerable style and was a notable bibliophile who surrounded himself with first editions and artworks. Unlike Northrup, Bixby was a highly cultured, intelligent and sophisticated man, whose riches and position had been accumulated entirely through his own efforts. He was now 64 years of age, white bearded and portly.

Understandably Northrup was keen to create a good impression during the visit. He wanted to demonstrate to this old family friend how he too had made a success of life (contrary to expectations). He was now Sir Northrup and Ukamba Member for the Legislative Council, a person of considerable importance in Kenya. Northrup enjoyed showing off to Bixby, the St Louisan Grandee, who was gratifyingly impressed by Northrup's elevated status and easy friendship with top officials and the cream of Kenyan society.

On 24th January 1921, the Bixby party, which included Bixby's wife Lillian and his son Donald as well as a Mrs Bell and her daughter Lucie Bell, steamed into Mombasa and anchored off Kilindini. Bixby spotted a little steam craft come out from shore and circling nearby the ship. He wrote in his diary that he immediately recognised "the slender figure of Sir Northrup on the back seat looking very fit and as if he still weighed the 330 lbs that he did last autumn."*181*

Northrup took them ashore and then to Mombasa Station to catch the train to Nairobi. He had been waiting in Mombasa for five days for the ship to arrive and had been staying at Likoni as a guest of Sir Ali bin Salim, the Sultan of Zanzibar's representative. Sir Northrup knew Sir Ali from the Legislative Council and told the suitably impressed Bixby that he stayed there whenever he came to Mombasa.[182]

Northrup had booked the best seats on the train for his guests in

---

181 Bixby Diary, 31.
182 Pilly Turner, personal interview. Sir Ali bin Salim had allowed Northrup to build himself a guesthouse on his land next door to him and after his death Lady McMillan still used it whenever she went down to the Coast.

the first carriage next to the engine and he travelled with them on the journey to Nairobi. He acted as tour guide describing the passing sights and explaining the main facts about the country – Kenya as it was now called, no longer British East Africa.

Bixby, the ex-foundry and railway man, noted the manufacture of the freight cars – mostly of steel-capacity as follows: 10 tons – 22400 pounds – 44800 pounds. He saw that the ties of the line were also of steel on account of the white ants, which destroyed the wooden ones.

Northrup, who had thought of everything for the comfort of his guests, presented Bixby with a personal servant called Mohamed. He was to be his personal 'boy' although as Bixby commented he was at least 35 years old, but he wrote: "I can see he will be very useful."[183]

The train still stopped for meals, which were taken at Dak bungalows along the route, and the journey to Nairobi took 24 hours, twelve hours shorter than Northrup's first journey in 1904. Bixby was enthralled by the travelling circus (as he called it) that he saw out of his window. He noted the different trees, the colourful people and the extraordinary wild life appearing so close to the train. Northrup kept up a running commentary, identifying each species of animal they saw and pointing out Mount Kilimanjaro, when it appeared floating above the clouds.

"At one station," Bixby wrote in his diary, "there were natives working changing grade of track and they called out as we passed 'Cigarro!' I threw out a half smoked cigar and it almost created a riot. Many of the natives wore ready made clothing, easily changed to fit different sizes, which consisted of old gunny sacks with holes punched through for head, arms and legs, though the younger ones were perhaps waiting for more gunny sacks as their only garment was a smile."[184]

Later on he wrote:

"3.25 we were at the station, where we found Lady Lucie,

183 Bixby Diary, 33.
184 Bixby Diary, 39.

handsome and charming as ever and no change at all, unless for the better, except grey hair."[185]

They then proceeded to Chiromo where they found Mr Bulpett – "the real English Gentleman"[186] – in residence, and living next door was Lucie's nephew Marcuswell Maxwell[187] – known as Max – his wife and small son, Peter.[188] He was helping to manage the McMillan's substantial land holdings. Bixby was taken on a tour of the spacious grounds of Chiromo and saw the stables and kennels. He admired Lucie's beautiful flower garden and her roses and reported that she kept 20 of her 60 horses at Chiromo as well as several dogs.

As January 25th was Burns Night, several glasses of whisky were drunk and toasts made to the Burns Club of St Louis, of which Bixby was an enthusiastic supporter.

The useful Mohamed waited on Bixby hand and foot. Mohamed laid out his clothes, helped him to dress, fixed the studs in his shirts and even tied his shoelaces.

"No one but a fat man appreciates how much assistance can be rendered. I expect if I lived here I should get used to it and permit him to do everything for me but eat," wrote Bixby in his diary.[189]

---

185 BixbyDiary., 40.
186 This was a slight dig at Northrup, who had become an English gentleman, having renounced his American citizenship, but of course retained his American mannerisms.
187 Marcuswell Maxwell (1890 –1938) was Lucie's nephew and the son of Lucie's elder sister Annie who had married Professor Walter Maxwell an Englishman in 1889. Max was married to Margaret Pugh the daughter of an Australian clergyman. His elder brother Clyde had been killed in France in World War I. Colonel Marcuswell Maxwell was a photographer of wildlife, whose pictures appeared in the Times Newspaper and was influential in the move to conserve wildlife. He died suddenly on April 21st 1938. He was badly affected by his war experience.
188 Clyde Fairbanks Peter Maxwell (1917-1983), known as Peter, eventually inherited the Kenyan properties on the death of Lucie McMillan.
189 Bixby Diary, 40.

Northrup introduced Bixby to Sir Charles Bowring,[190] Chief Secretary of the Colony, and Bowring's wife along with Judge Barth, the chief justice of Kenya, who were invited round to dinner and a game of bridge. Later Bixby met Carl Akeley, the American sculptor and naturalist, who came to tea along with an authoress called Mary Hastings Bradley and her six-year-old daughter. Akeley had just returned from an expedition amongst the gorillas in northern Uganda and was eager to tell them of his experiences. Interestingly the large male gorilla weighed only a few more pounds that his host, Northrup. Mr Frayne also came to call, a mining expert who was advising Northrup on his latest project – a gold mine. Major Grogan dropped by on another day. Next door the Maxwells arranged a dance for the young people. It all sounded extraordinarily cosy and friendly in the McMillan circle.

Bixby was then taken on a tour of the extensive landholdings owned by the McMillans in Kenya. First of all he visited Mua, a 14,000 acre farm at Machakos, where Lucie raised cattle, horses and pigs and made cheddar cheese and butter. There was an orchard there as well with a fine crop of red plums. Northrup told Bixby the story of how he had acquired the farm. Lord Delamere and he had gone halves on the land, bought from an entrepreneurial missionary called Stewart Watts, who was leaving the country. Not long after Northrup had finalised his purchase from Watts, he was visited by a representative of the CMS Mission, who had come out from England to take possession of the land vacated by Watts. But as Watts had put his own name on the title deed, he was legally the owner and the Mission did not have a leg stand on, and so lost out. Apparently Watts went back to England, joined another Mission and acquired another farm by this means. His son, described by Northrup "as conscienceless as the father" had inherited it and was now farming close to McMillan's farm at Donyo Sabuk.

Bixby then visited their flax farm at Kikuyu and some woodland they owned at Ngong. The biggest land holding was at Donyo Sabuk,

---

190 He had worked closely with Bowring on the War Council and Bowring had deputised as Governor of Kenya during the 22-month interregnum before Northey was appointed. Northrup must have known him well.

McMillan's Ol Donyo Sabuk house under construction in 1921.

consisting of 35,000 acres, according to Bixby.[191] It was an hour and half's drive from Nairobi. Here McMillan not only owned the mountain, but had started growing sisal on farmland purchased to the north of it.[192] He had disposed of his 19,000 acre Juja Farm by this stage. Northrup showed Bixby the large new house he was building at Donyo Sabuk.

It was built with the grey local stone and was a rambling single storey bungalow. It had six bedrooms, a large dining room, living room and spacious hall, besides a kitchen extension and verandas overlooking the plains and the mountains. Bixby noted the beams in the dining room and how the roof covered with galvanised iron had thatch woven above it to keep it cool.

---

191 Bixby Diary, 44.

192 Rumour had it that the land had been won in a poker game from the former owners Penton and Bunbury. Many years later Dick Daniel, who worked at Donyo Sabuk farm, remembers a rather sad looking hut, which was always known as Bunbury's – so one can only imagine that the farm was not in good shape when it was acquired by Northrup. According to Mary Gillett (1986) *Tribute to Pioneers; Index of many of the Pioneers of East Africa* Harry H Penton, who settled in Kenya in 1904, originally farmed 5,000 acres at Donyo Sabuk. He was an importer of thoroughbred horses and owned some of the best racehorses in the country in the early years. Vesturme R W Bunbury a Captain of the East African Rifles came to Kenya in 1899. He resigned his commission and took up farming at Donyo Sabuk. Some time later he moved to Lake Naivasha where sailing and boatbuilding became his chief interest.

Regel, Northrup's cook from his time in Sudan, who was formerly at Juja, presided over the kitchen.[193]

At Donyo Sabuk Bixby was given his first taste of hunting in Africa. He was taken for a spin in Northrup's new hunting Cadillac. Recently imported from the US, this had the sides cut down so Northrup could shoot while sitting in the vehicle. Owen the chauffeur drove Bixby and Northrup round Ol Donyo Sabuk looking for something suitable to shoot. Eventually they came upon a herd of impala. They drove up, Northrup took aim and hit one, and then let out his bull terrier, Bettie, who ran and dragged the wounded animal to the car. Owen drew out his knife and cut its throat and tied the carcass to the side of the car. The successful hunters returned with their kill.

This was the epitome of a lazy man's style of hunting, requiring virtually no effort. It was quite different from traditional hunting practise, which was done on foot or on horseback. Here there was no tracking or patient skill involved. The hunter simply drove his car at speed over the rough ground amongst a herd and took pot shots with his large and expensive gun, which could kill at 350 yards, never moving off his seat. However, to give Northrup his due, he did not shoot indiscriminately in this instance, but chose carefully one impala, as it had the best meat, for dinner, and he was on his own land.[194]

Later, concerns would be raised about this method of hunting. The fashion for hunting with cars decimated wild life ever more efficiently and eliminated much of the skill and mystique associated with the sport.

---

193 Regel the cook was a Somali, who had been the chief cook on McMillan's second expedition in 1904. According to Jessen he was always cheerful, always smiling and full of fun with a strange use of the English language, which caused much amusement. His family had been raided by the Mahdist army, when they lost everything, and he was, consequently, very anti the Mahdi.Burchard Heinrich Jessen, *W N McMillan's Expeditions and Big Game Hunting in Sudan, Abyssinia and British East Africa* (1906), 111.

194 As Northrup was too heavy to ride a horse, previously he had used his buckboard for hunting. The skilful Michael and his Kikuyu assistant could manoeuvre it like a Roman chariot chasing after game at breakneck speed over the Athi plains. Edward Stewart White gives a good description of the exciting hunt he had with Northrup in his mule cart, in his book *Land of Footprints* (1913), 377.

New ideas for conservation laws and game parks for wildlife protection were just starting in Kenya in response to fears of over-hunting and extinction of rare species. A revulsion against the orgy of killing on some hunting safaris was also beginning to find expression. In 1928 Denys Finch-Hatton, himself a professional hunter, called for a total ban on hunting with cars and wrote articles in praise of photographing animals rather than killing them. He claimed that shooting wildlife with a camera rather than with a gun, could be just as enjoyable and exhilarating. Marcuswell Maxwell, Lucie's nephew, was a talented wildlife photographer and it was his pictures of lions, which inspired Finch Hatton to speak out and begin the serious debate on how to regulate the safari industry.[195]

That however was still in the future and on February 7th McMillan started out on an extended hunting safari. The initial group consisted of Max and Margaret Maxwell together with Canon and Mrs Pugh, Margaret's parents, as well as Northrup, Lucie, Bulpett, Bixby, Lillian, Donald and Mrs and Miss Bell– 12 persons in all.

They set out in four vehicles: two Cadillacs, Northrup's special hunting Cadillac and Lucie's Cadillac for the ladies; and two 'Overlanders,' one carrying the Maxwells and the other with Bulpett, Donald and the servants. A caravan of five ox-driven wagons had been sent ahead 10 days previously, carrying all the tents and provisions. There was also a separate water cart. Each wagon had 18 bullocks to haul it and the drivers carried long rhino whips, which cracked like a rifle shot.

Northrup did not believe in travelling light and this safari was no exception to his rule. The camp was enormous consisting of at least twenty tents. Each tent took two people and Lucie and Donald had their own single tents. In addition, there was the mess tent, the store tent with the guns, separate WC tents for men and women, a cook's tent and tents for servants, gunbearers and skinners. All the tents had ditches dug around them in case of rain. At the back of each tent there was an annex for canvas washbasins on sticks and the canvas bathtub on the

195 Sara Wheeler, *Too Close to the Sun* (2006), 204.

ground, which was filled with three inches of hot water at the end of each day. With such elaborate amenities the camp could only move a maximum 13 miles a day. Life in McMillan's camp was truly luxurious with servants at the ready, plentiful food and the campfire ritual after nightfall, when stories were told and liquor drunk.

Lucie and Northrup by this stage seemed to have divided their lives along clearly delineated lines of his and hers. Each had their own Cadillac, Mua farm was described as Lucie's farm, while Donyo Sabuk was Northrup's. Unlike the other couples on the safari, they did not share a tent. Lucie had her own tent, while Northrup shared with Bulpett – as noted by Bixby in his diary. Bulpett was still a firm fixture in the McMillan household, but his exact role was never clearly defined. He appeared to act as a go-between husband and wife, perhaps providing the equilibrium for the marriage to work.

They camped on the edge of the Maasai Reserve and hoped to see lion but were unsuccessful. They shot topi, wildebeest and Thomson's gazelles and saw jackals and hyenas in profusion but despite sitting up two nights in homemade bomas, no lions came. They tried baiting the lions with carcasses of zebra and wildebeest, which smelt dreadful – but the lions were unimpressed and failed to come. Canon and Mrs Pugh took photographs of Maasai warriors and enjoyed the scenery. After a week on safari, the ladies, the Canon, Max and Bulpett left for Nairobi. Donald, Northrup and Bixby went on in search of lions.

They met up with Judd, the professional hunter, who told them they'd find lions past Narok, near Ndelele. Northrup had hoped to engage Judd for their safari, but he had a prior commitment. They travelled on to Narok and paid a courtesy call on the DC (District Commissioner), Colonel Barrett, who was an old friend of Northrup's.[196] Barrett discussed the Maasai problem, saying how the Maasai were becoming a decadent race, as the young warriors were no longer the fine fighting men they had been before WWI, when they used to raid and attack other tribes. The new rules and regulations of the Colonial Government

196 William Edward Hawkes Barrett first came to Kenya in 1902 and served with the KAR, but joined the Provincial Administration in 1906. He knew the country well and was an experienced and long standing official.

had curtailed much of the Maasai traditional warlike activities and the tribe had suffered accordingly in his opinion. He also mentioned that unlike other tribes in Kenya the Maasai had not joined the army to help fight the war.

Bixby was interested to see how the Maasai oiled themselves and rubbed red soil on their heads and body to colour their skin a brick red. He was told they did not eat vegetables but lived on a diet of meat and blood mixed with milk from their cattle. The young warriors carried a short sword and long heavy spear, which was used to kill the lions and leopards, which might threaten their cattle. They did not use anything on their weapons, unlike the Akamba who coated their arrows with a type of poison found in the woods on Ol Donyo Sabuk, according to Northrup. After leaving the District Commissioner they visited an Indian store where they stocked up on provisions.

Once the ladies had gone home, Northrup's manners become more relaxed. On a couple of occasions Bixby described Northrup losing his temper and swearing at his servants if they failed to do his bidding. At one point he gave a wagon driver a hard kick, sending him flying into a bush, for disobeying his instructions. He became less polite in all male company and discussed the sexual habits of various tribes and thought it a good joke when Bixby was reluctant to be photographed holding hands with a young Maasai girl. Northrup had himself photographed hand in hand with the girl, but Bixby stood self-consciously with the girl's hand just resting on his arm. When she demanded one rupee for each photograph, Northrup ungenerously refused and gave her one for both.[197]

Later when they were trying to find a suitable site to set up camp, one of the Indian storekeepers, Mr Singh, came running up in distress. He

197 Black and white segregation was still very strict in USA at this period especially in the Southern States. Missouri had been a slave state until 1865. Being photographed holding hands with a black African was still anathema to many older Americans – Bixby could not quite bring himself to do it. Northrup now British and a Kenyan settler had become more relaxed about colour and was happy to hold hands with the Maasai girl. A colour bar operated in Kenya until the 1950s but it was never as rigidly enforced or as deeply entrenched as in the USA.

Northrup McMillan near Narok taking the testimony from the Indian trader Mr Singh after his store was robbed and his African employee was murdered.

claimed he had been robbed the night before and his African employee, who had been sent with a message to his brother, had disappeared, feared murdered. The Indian took them to a spot where bloodstains could be seen on the path and they followed the trail of blood until they came upon the body of an African impaled with a short Maasai sword.

Northrup took the testimony of the Indian trader and wrote out an account of the murder and gave it to Mr Singh to take back to the DC, Colonel Barrett. Northrup's position as a Member of Leg Co and a magistrate gave him the right to hold impromptu court hearings and take witness statements, which much impressed Bixby. He recorded the example of Kenyan justice working in the field and photographed Northrup taking the statement from the Indian trader.

Now camped at Ndelele in lion country they spent two weeks sitting up every night with an extremely smelly and rotting carcass as bait, waiting for lions to make an appearance. Two of them would sit in the cage, a contraption especially constructed as a mobile hide, while the others took it in turns in the hunting car camouflaged with foliage. It was a cold and uncomfortable operation. One person stayed awake, watching the different coloured eyes glowing in the dark and listening for tell tale signs of lion, gun at the ready, while the other catnapped as best he could, until the agreed signal came – a punch in the thigh. One night when Northrup and Bixby were sharing a night vigil in the car, Northup carelessly threw down the butt of his lighted cigarette into the dry undergrowth and nearly set his Cadillac on fire. The potentially dangerous situation was saved by emptying the contents of their water bottles onto the smouldering grass and damping it down with their bare hands until all sparks were extinguished. No lions were seen that night.

In the end patience was rewarded. Bixby and Donald each got a lion as well as a leopard and they had themselves proudly photographed with their kill draped beside them. The McMillan lion hunt appeared to be a tiring and messy business, not at all like the glamorous lion hunts portrayed by Selous and others in their famous hunting books. But Northrup was determined not to allow his guests to return without bagging a lion. The elderly and fastidious Bixby was quite relieved when camp was at last struck and they returned to the comforts of Chiromo and a good night's sleep.

After the safari, they rested a couple of nights at Chiromo and met up with the Greswolde-Williams, whose farm they had passed on their way at the start of their hunting trip. The McMillans had called in and left their visiting card, but found the Williams away and now the call was being returned, as was polite custom in society of the day.

They then spent a further few days at Donyo Sabuk, where they discovered the house more fully furnished than previously and the garden and access road being cleared.

Bixby admired the oak style furniture inside and recognised William McMillan's old desk in one corner by the huge fireplace. Lucie told him that she planned to decorate the walls of the living areas with Maasai shields and spears.

McMillan's Donyo Sabuk house still stands today and is virtually unchanged from when it was built. The area is now called Kangundo in Matungulu district. Pilly Turner, who came to Donyo Sabuk in 1927 as a child, remembers the fine Edwardian furnishings and the

The rear of Ol Donyo Sabuk house undergoing repairs in 2010.

enormous armchair in the sitting room reserved for Sir Northrup. In the dining room there was a long table, which could seat at least 16, and one of the bedrooms was 'Charles' room' for Charles Bulpett, the funny little old man who always accompanied Lady McMillan on her visits.[198]

During World War II Lady McMillan lent the house to the government as a military convalescent home, and it was used to house the Duke of Aosta, Commander in Chief of the defeated Italian forces in Ethiopia and his retinue. Dick Daniell, who came to work for Lady McMillan from 1948-1954 as a field assistant, remembered staying there when he first arrived. He recalled how the spacious hallway, which went through the house, opened on to large windows, which provided views over the mountain and toward Machakos. He says the furnishings were old fashioned and there was even a suit of armour near the main door. He had to move out for Lady McMillan's Christmas Party, when several houseguests were expected, but the party in fact was cancelled when the water pump, which brought water from the dam, broke down. In later years, Lady McMillan used the house only occasionally for entertaining and lived mainly in Nairobi at Chiromo.[199] On her death the house was sold and after independence it became the headquarters of a farmer's cooperative. Nowadays the original stonework is covered in white concrete cladding and the manicured grounds have long disappeared, but the structure is unmistakable. Donyo Sabuk house is a long and rambling bungalow. It is an informal country property and

198 Pilly Turner, personal interview. Pilly is the, daughter of Jack Everard, manager at Donyo Sabuk.
199 Dick Daniell, personal interview.

is slightly disappointing as a work of architecture. It does not have the elegant style of Chiromo, nevertheless it is an important house, with a wealth of interesting history.[200] It was gazetted as a national monument in 2008 and is now owned by the Government of Kenya and is currently under restoration.

African workers dig the garden at Northrup's Donyo Sabuk house.

During Bixby's visit, Northrup told his guests of the legend attached to the Mountain, Ol Donyo Sabuk. Long ago the Kikuyu owned and occupied the mountain, but later the Akamba tribe took it from them. There was said to be an enormous cave under the mountain where the Kikuyu would take refuge whenever the Maasai or Akamba people threatened them. The cave was so large that they would drive all their goats and cattle into it and stay there until danger was past. There was also supposed to be a spring of water inside the cave. Northrup said he had never managed to find this cave, but he believed that if the mountain was mined, diamonds, garnets and white sapphire would be found.

Sitting on the veranda, Bixby noticed how Ol Donyo Sabuk had a three colour striped appearance, with the dark woods at the top, a bright green in the middle from a band of wild currant bushes, and the pale brownish swathe of the plains at the bottom. The Bixby party drove to the summit and admired the view from all sides, and in the evening enjoyed the peace and quiet of the African countryside, contemplated the stars and identified the Southern Cross twinkling high up in the heavens.

---

200 The story that is frequently told of how McMillan being in a hurry to get his house built offered the fundi a bonus to finish it on time probably refers to this house, rather than Juja. The fundi got his bonus, it is said, but at the expense of a few crooked walls – some of the walls in the early photographs of Donyo Sabuk look distinctly crooked.

The Bixby's expected departure was delayed so they decided to visit Lake Victoria and Uganda. Northrup and Lucie drove their guests via Lake Navaisha, Gilgil and Nakuru stopping at a hotel in Eldoret. The next day as they entered Kavirondo (Luo) country. Bixby was surprised to see how heavily populated it was, more so than any area they had so far seen. The travellers admired the round grass huts, where the people lived cultivating bananas and corn, and wearing very few clothes. Northrup told Bixby that he liked the Kavirondo (Luo) people as he thought them hard working and said that they were responding well to western education and were making great strides.[201] Later they crossed Lake Victoria by ferry and saw the Ripon Falls and Jinja.

On their return to Nairobi, March 17th, Bixby noted in his diary that there had been a native riot in Nairobi led by a Kikuyu called Harry Thuku, who had been raised and educated by missionaries. Bixby wrote in his diary that Thuku had been employed by the Government's Treasury Department, but he had been arrested for forgery and had been jailed for several months. After his release, he commenced propaganda against the British, "rather like Gandhi," according to Bixby. On March 16th he had been arrested again and put in police quarters not far from Chiromo[202] and his supporters had demonstrated in protest and marched 3,000 strong to the police headquarters. Six representatives had gone to the Governor and asked for his release but this had been refused. The riot had then worsened and KAR troops were called to the scene of the troubles, where the demonstrators had thrown stones at them. The troops had then opened fire and killed some of the demonstrators, who only then finally dispersed.[203]

---

201 Dick Daniell, personal interview. Most of Northrup's workers on his sisal estate were Luos. No Kikuyu were employed, but there were some Akamba.
202 He was detained at the Nairobi Police Lines alongside the Norfolk Hotel.
203 Harry Thuku was the founder of the East African Association, the first African political group to campaign against the colonial regime in Kenya. He demanded a stop to the theft of native land, a living wage, and an end to forced labour, the hut tax and the kipande. He was eventually exiled to the NFD and the handling of this riot, when 25 demonstrators were shot dead, is often cited as an example of the worst excesses of the Kenyan Colonial Government in the period between the wars.

Bixby made a note in his diary about nicknames.[204] Northrup's African name was Mkoro – meaning 'the man of many cattle.' (A less complimentary meaning was possibly the man who has trouble breathing or 'the wheezer,' a reference to his bronchial problem. This meaning was not recorded by Bixby.)[205] Bulpett's African name was Mzee: Old Man. (This again has a meaning open to a dual- interpretation as it can also mean the one in over-all charge as Africans have great respect for age.)

On 22nd March Bixby and his wife dined at Government House with the McMillans. Here they met the Governor, Lord Northey and his wife, and sat 26 at dinner.[206] Northey showed Bixby his pet cheetah[207] and at dinner the conversation was all about the Indian troubles. Northey accused the Indians of being behind the Thuku riot and deliberately stirring up the young mission-educated Africans.

The next day the Bixby's returned to Government House to register their names in the Government House book. They met Northey again by accident, and he took them to see his trophies and collection of skins. This was their last day in Nairobi and they left by train to Mombasa

204 Bixby Diary, 84. Nearly all European settlers were given nicknames by their staff, and quite often they were not complimentary, picking up on a physical characteristic or habit.

205 The intended meaning of McMillan's African nickname has always been the subject of some speculation. Mkoro has been translated variously: as the man who has to spit sideways, or as the man who has so many houses he doesn't know which to call his home. Pilly Turner told me that Lucie McMillan was called Memsahib Mkoro by her African staff.

206 Elspeth Huxley, *The Mottled Lizard* (1962), 93. "A small dapper fierce and monocled General, who had fought in East Africa during the war. His fierceness was a shell. He was actually a man of kindness and goodwill. Although he seemed to some of the farmers rather stuck-up and formal, and was a stickler for proto-col, they respected him because he knew his mind and spoke it and because they believed in his sincerity. In his home life he was overshadowed by a forceful, high-spirited and outspoken wife from the Cape and by three attractive, independent and ebullient daughters, with whom a great many men were always in love."

207 ibid, 65. Northey's pet cheetah had the freedom of the house and had once sent a visiting grandee's lady into hysterics when it met her on the stairs. It used to jump onto the table during meetings of his Executive Council, scattering docu-ments of state with a tail lashing in affection.

that evening. Northrup, Bulpett and Lucie came to the station to wave their final goodbyes.

According to Bixby, Northrup had been an excellent host, and the safari experience had been unforgettable. He wrote in his diary: "I have the floating bone, or trophy bone of a big lion and two of my leopard to prove it is real and our camps at Mt Ciswa and Ndelele will never be forgotten. Northrup always gave me the chance for a shot in preference to himself and as a host he cannot be improved upon. He is the same fine manly fellow he always has been and his title has not changed him or Lucie in the slightest."[208]

Northrup had certainly entertained the Bixby party royally for a good two months.

---

208 Bixby Diary, 71.

CHAPTER XII

THE FINAL YEARS

In late autumn the lilac flowers of the jacaranda trees were in full glory and their petals festooned the streets of Nairobi. These colourful trees were imported from Brazil in about 1910. The seedlings flourished in the soil and climate of Nairobi and were planted wherever the settlers built their houses, in avenues and in gardens. Ten years on the trees had matured and blossomed and the town was taking shape with proper roads, shops and offices – a 'green city in the sun.' It now took just over an hour to drive to Thika, 32 miles from Nairobi, on the straight and newly tarmacadamed Government Road.

Northrup had lost heart in his farming experiments at Juja. He'd tried ostriches, cattle, pigs, coffee and you name it, but none of them had proved successful despite the effort and the money he had thrown at them, and the war years had been a disaster. Ostrich feathers were no longer worn, coffee export had been banned during the war as an unnecessary luxury, the value of flax had plummeted and his pigs and cattle had failed to thrive. Northrup sold his dairy herd and Juja farm in 1921 at a knock down price. The exact reason for the sale is not known, but Juja was no longer the hunter's paradise it once had been. The teeming wildlife of the early days was much diminished, depredated by hunting safaris and by increased settlement in the area. Also in 1921-1922 Northrup was involved in a protracted court case suing his manager at Juja for mishandling the care of his farm and his dairy herd. This may have caused Northrup to give up on Juja and was probably the reason why Lucie's nephew Max Maxwell was brought in to oversee the McMillan Estates, and to help Northrup in the day-to-day running of his farms. Northrup turned his attention to land he had acquired further to the north of Ol Donyo Sabuk, which was more easily accessible by road and built a new house closer to the mountain.

Northrup also had a new interest – gold mining. He had tried earlier in 1905 to find gold in the Blue Nile, but the expert he had hired had failed and had almost died in the search. The gold they had found was not in sufficient quantities to be financially viable. Northrup had abandoned the idea of gold mining. But in the 1920s, prospecting for gold fired his imagination again. He purchased mining rights at Lolgorien Hill in the Maasai Reserve. Fools Gold or iron pyrites, washed into the alluvial mud and found in pools, was often mistaken for gold, but he was assured by expert opinion

McMillan's traction engine used for ploughing
and bringing sisal to the factory at Donyo Sabuk.

Sisal plants at Donyo Sabuk with the manager E L Lindsay (right) and his wife (centre).

that the gold at Lolgorien was the real thing. He set up a company, Kenya Gold Mining Syndicate Ltd, and persuaded his friends to buy shares in his goldmine. Bixby when he visited in 1921 contributed $1,000. He commented in his diary that he doubted he would ever see a return. He knew Northrup well and his history of bold schemes that inevitably disappointed! The mineral wealth in Kenya, unlike South Africa or Rhodesia, was known to be poor but Northrup was confident there was more hidden underground than people thought. He pressed for the mining laws to be relaxed, for licences to be more easily obtained and land release for mining exploration made easier. He spoke on the Legislative Council on the subject and sat on a commission set up to review the mining act in Kenya.

Like the adventurers of King Solomon's Mines he dreamt of finding gold and untold riches in Africa. He believed that his own mountain Ol Donyo Sabuk contained precious stones[209] and was certain that an investment in Lolgorien would prove lucrative. There was no road to Lolgorien, so one had to be made to transport mining equipment to the area. The newly constructed bridge over the river collapsed when a herd of elephants walked over it, causing yet more delay. Despite these setbacks Northrup remained determinedly optimistic. In the Kenya Gazette for July 1924 a notice appeared granting two prospecting licences to Sir Northrup McMillan for six months from 11th July over a total area of 10 miles near Lolgorien Hill in the Maasai Reserve. True to form, Lolgorien Mine failed to produce gold during Northrup's

---

209 Pilly Turner, personal interview. Pilly, the daughter of Jack Everard, Lady McMillan's manager at Donyo Sabuk, remembers digging and finding garnets on the mountain.

lifetime, but the area is still mined today and produces small amounts of artesian gold, while the mining laws were eventually rewritten.

The McMillans were now part of high society in Nairobi. They dined with the Governor and were on easy terms with the top officials.[210] They knew everyone who was anyone. Lucie ordered a new dinner set, complete with baronial crest, and the champagne dinners at Chiromo became more elaborate and the guests more illustrious. In the diaries of Lord Francis Scott, now at Rhodes House, there are several mentions of dinners with the McMillans often followed by a game of bridge. Lord Francis Scott was the younger son of the Duke of Buccleuch, who had married Eileen daughter of Lord Minto, former viceroy of India, and so was at the very pinnacle of Kenyan society. He had been badly wounded in the war and came to Kenya on the Soldier Settler scheme in 1919 to farm. In 1920-1921 he was working hard setting up his farm and building the house prior to bringing out his wife and daughter. Whenever he visited Nairobi for race week or to watch the cricket match Settlers v Officials, the McMillans would invite him over to dine at Chiromo. He particularly liked Lucie and appreciated the excellent food served at their table by an English butler. He commented in his diary, "They are Americans but naturalised British now." Afterwards they would sometimes adjourn to the Muthaiga Club and on one occasion he described a riotous evening when there were steeple-chasing races over the chairs and sofas. Mrs Grant and Mrs Birkbeck won the ladies' race, he recorded.

Lady McMillan was elected Chair of the East African Women's League (EAWL) in 1921 and in 1922, when the EAWL was experiencing financial difficulties, Sir Northrup and Lady McMillan came to its rescue with an interest free loan so that the library, restroom and produce exchange could be kept open and the rent paid. This was

---

210 John Sutton, personal interview. One tale about Lady McMillan, which illustrates just how influential they had become, tells of how she complained to the Governor about being disturbed at night by railway trains passing between Ainsworth Bridge and the cutting leading towards Westlands, and that, as a result, the line from Nairobi station to Western Kenya was re-laid around Kibera to Dagoretti.

later converted into an outright gift. The EAWL, Kenya's version of the WI (Women's Institute), did valuable work in the colony, donating to charities such as the Red Cross, running an employment agency and giving help to battered or deserted European wives. The library was a central meeting place and the 'bring and buy' sales were very popular.[211]

Lady McMillan won prizes for her roses, showed her dogs and kept racehorses, while Northrup was much in demand for committee work. The Red Book for 1922 lists him as Steward of the Jockey club of Kenya, Vice-President Makuyu Hunt Club, Vice President Nairobi Polo Club, Member

Photograph of Lady Lucie McMillan in 1921 when she was chairman of the East African Women's League.

of the Education Board, President of the Ulu Farmers Association, Machakos and President of the EASPCA. He continued to enjoy a drink at the Muthaiga Club, where he was also on the committee and when at Donyo Sabuk would patronise The Blue Posts Hotel next to the picturesque Chania Falls at Thika. It was here at a poker game he is supposed to have won his sisal farm at Donyo Sabuk from the former owners. Sisal originally came from Mexico and grew well on the dry plains. The plants took three years to reach maturity and needed a large labour force to harvest successfully, so a considerable capital outlay was needed before any profit from the crop could be realised. Northrup was in the fortunate position of having plenty of cash to spare, and by 1924 had a large area under cultivation. He had installed a small steam traction engine running on more than ten miles of track, which carried the sisal to the factory where the leaves were stripped and processed

---

211 The EAWL was started in 1917 in Nairobi and the Bank of Baroda now stands on the site of the old library building, its first headquarters.

for the fibre.[212]

A satirical sketch of Sir Northrup McMillan appeared in *The Critic* newspaper dated 27th February 1923. Nora Strange had been writing amusing cameos of the chief notables of Nairobi in her column entitled 'In the Limelight' and Northrup appeared as No.8. Both Grogan and Delamere had been portrayed earlier in the series.[213] The light-hearted satire of Northrup began with a spot of doggerel verse:

> Halloa! How's everybody?
> Fine weather for the ducks Eh?
> My name's Sir N McMillan
> As you know I'm always willin
> To do a bit of good for any man
> I'm a sport, the people tell me,
> but my own desires compel me
> to give a little help whene'er I can
> Then at politics I'm splendid
> and when rights must be defended
> I'm up and at 'em quietly but with vim
> I am solid and I'm steady
> Not excitable nor heady
> Its always "there's Sir Northrup. Go to him"

It goes on to mention his fondness for champagne dinners and the new diet he is on – special thinning water to be taken with meals. He had just bought himself a scooter for getting around Nairobi, which provides an excuse for some more fun: "Ha! Ha! I do look some guy! Its' all me and no scooter, I fairly overflow the little thing." His gold prospecting gets a mention and of course his wealth and title, which inspires the writer to break out into some more rhyming verse.

---

212 Most of the labour employed were Luo, and Tom Mboya, the well-known Kenyan politician, was born on the estate, though after Northrup McMillan had died.

213 Nora Strange first wrote 'Potted Personalities A Masque of Modern Nairobi' for the Star & Garter Hospital fete in 1918, but later she expanded on the original idea and wrote them up as separate articles for *The Critic*.

I often think a good stunt would be for me to go off big game
hunting again and get out of all the worries of owning pots of
money. It is a responsibility I can tell you.
Still I'll stay and face the trouble
After all, life's just a bubble
And what's the use of worrying Eh what?
And really it is funny
When you've got a bit of money
Surprising what a lot of friends you've got
When you add to cash, a title...

It is gentle lampooning and obviously Northrup and Lucie took it
all in good part as the complete text was stuck in their scrapbook.

Amongst the McMillans' closest friends was Karen Blixen. She
was a snob and only mixed with aristocrats or those she felt were on
the same cultural level.   Karen Blixen had first met the McMillans
at Juja in December 1917, when
she and Bror were invited for a
hunting expedition. Karen, who
was suspected of being pro-German
earlier on, was now deemed
acceptable when it was learnt that
her brother had received the VC
(Victoria Cross) medal[214] and was
fighting on the British side. Lady
McMillan appears to have taken a
particular liking to Karen, though
Karen wrote in one of her earlier
letters that she preferred Northrup.
They had much in common; both
women were interested in art, music

Northrup McMillan in his later years.

---

214 Awarded for conspicuous bravery, it was the most prestigious honour handed
out to a member of the armed forces in Britain. Many were awarded posthumous-
ly.

and literature and liked elegant dressing and elaborate entertaining. When Karen fell from her horse and developed blood poisoning, she stayed at Chiromo as a guest of the McMillans to convalesce.[215] She borrowed their books and enjoyed reading Uncle Bulpett's French novels. During the Bixby visit in 1921, the McMillan party met up with Karen by chance at the Muthaiga Club and offered to drive her home to the farm. Bixby the connoisseur enjoyed the opportunity of seeing Karen's fine furniture and paintings, which she had brought out from Denmark. The McMillans felt sorry for her as her husband, Bror, by this time had left her and the farm was in dire straits. Perhaps Northrup even felt a twinge of guilt, as it was his Swedo African Coffee farm, part owned with Aage Sjogren, which Bror had unwisely bought back in 1913.

It is probable that Northrup lent Karen money on occasions and when he went round to drink tea with her, she would put an extra large chair out on the veranda for him to sit in. In her letters she described how despite his enormous bulk, he moved gracefully and was curiously light on his feet. She admired Northrup's courtly manners and she put him in one of her short stories, using him as a model for Prince Potenziani in the story, entitled *The Roads around Pisa*.[216] She sent her mother a newspaper clipping of herself with Northrup, arm in arm. He is wearing what looks like a baseball cap and looks immense and baggy beside the slender white clad figure of Karen Blixen.[217]

Charles Bulpett, still living at Chiromo with the McMillans, was also a frequent visitor and a welcome addition at the Blixen dinner parties. Karen

215 Karen Blixen, letter to her mother, October 1918.

216 Judith Thurman, *The Life of Karen Blixen* (1982), 181. The book *Seven Gothic Tales* was published in 1934 and the one with Prince Potenziani tells the story of the tragic outcome of a misunderstanding. The Prince who is impotent and fearing his wife will demand an annulment, secretly employs his friend count Nino to take his place in the marital bed. But unknown to him the wife substitutes a friend in her place. The prince then blames Count Nino for failing to impregnate his wife as agreed and they have a duel and the Prince is killed.

217 Isak Dinesen, *Letters from Africa 1914-1931*, translated by Anne Born (1982).This photo was first taken at the garden party for the 'Star and Garter' Fund in September 1918 and is reproduced in Isak Dinesen's book.

enjoyed the way he could talk on any frivolous subject and she described him as "a virtuoso at the art of living." His mastery of the art of conversation made sure there were no embarrassing silences or pregnant pauses and his presence kept the small talk flowing. He was always active and cheerful in manner although by now over seventy.[218]

Illustrating just how close Lady McMillan and Karen became, is the famous incident when Karen's lover Denys Finch Hatton crashed his plane and was killed in 1931. Karen was due to lunch with Lady McMillan and some friends at Chiromo, and though the others in the room knew about the fatal accident, Karen did not. With great decorum and restraint they all ate lunch and carried on as if all was normal. Only afterwards did Lady McMillan draw Karen gently into another room and tell her the sad news.[219]

The McMillans were exceptionally kind to Karen and took her under their wing. She was something of an outsider and not popular with the other settlers, who thought her cold and affected. There are numerous references to the McMillans in her letters. In August 1922 she spent a weekend at Donyo Sabuk with Denys Finch Hatton and in October 1922 she was invited to dinner at Chiromo to meet the new Governor, Sir Robert Coryndon, and attended another lunch there in December 1923. When Fru Ingebord Dinesen, Karen's mother visited and stayed a couple of months from November 1924 until 12th January 1925, they drove out altogether and socialised nearly every day. Lady McMillan went with Karen to say goodbye to her mother at Nairobi Station when she left and afterwards dragged her to Chiromo to cheer her up. According to a letter written

---

218 Karen Blixen was fond of Bulpett as he reminded her of her own Uncle Laurentzius. She put him in her famous book *Out of Africa* (1937), where he featured as the narrator's great friend and "a kind of ideal to me." He was also used as one of the models for the courtly but impractical Baron von Brackel who narrates Karen's short story entitled: 'The old Chevalier,' *Seven Gothic Tales* (1934). It is a tale about a failed love affair and she describes the Baron as someone "who had travelled much and known many cities and men, but who had shown very little skill in managing his own affairs." Judith Thurman, *The Life of Karen Blixen* (1982), 181, describes Bulpett as the McMillan's permanent houseguest and a retired 'homme du monde.'

219 Judith Thurman, The Life of Karen Blixen (1982), 287.

by Karen to her mother on 14th January, "Lady McMillan tore me away before you had quite vanished. It is probably an English superstition that one should not see the last glimpse of someone."[220] In March 1925 Karen sailed to Europe having arranged to meet up with the McMillans in Paris.

A picture of what life was like in the 1920s in Kenya and a description of an event attended by Northrup McMillan comes from Elspeth Huxley in her book *The Mottled Lizard*. This continues the tale of her life in Kenya after World War I and contains an account of the Christmas Festivities and the New Year McMillan Polo Cup competition held at Makuyu in 1922.[221] Northrup McMillan had sponsored the competition and presented the cup named after him to the winning team.

> When a number of farmers in our district made plans to gather at Makuyu over Christmas they decided to put up bandas to house everyone who came. You made a banda by tying sisal poles together with strips of bark and arranging bundles of dry grass to make the walls and roof. You left a gap for the door way and perhaps a window aperture. The grass, poles and bark were free and so the only expense was the labour; and a good gang could run up several in a day. Bandas therefore appeared very quickly at Makuyu to shelter the farmers, their ponies and their ponies' syces, one syce to each animal. This was a custom imported, we understood from India. Africans soon got the hang of it and no syce would look after more than one pony. His duties were light, and his status superior.

> After the Christmas party had been fixed the rains came back, entirely out of season, and turned the whole plain into a soggy treacherous waterlogged morass. The mud, the leaking thatch, the sodden state of everything was taken as a joke, at least for the first day or so. A polo tournament was arranged for a cup presented by Sir Northrup McMillan; teams arrived from several districts, more ponies than I had ever seen at

---

220 Isak Dinesen, *Letters from Africa 1914-1931* (1982), 227-228.
221 Elspeth Huxley, *The Mottled Lizard* (1962), 132-135.

one time were assembled…We all brought our own food and camp equipment and fed in a communal banda furnished with trestle tables. Some of the players had scarcely wielded a stick before and few of the ponies knew what they were up to, but polo is a simple game in essence, started in Persia by posses of warriors riding at each other – and the Kenya version, though played by only four-a-side with one ball, must have somewhat resembled this embryonic form.

Every afternoon it poured with rain, the camp became a mass of slithery mud, people played bridge, moving their chairs about to avoid the drips, sang and drank whisky to keep out the cold.

She goes on to describe how after the Christmas Day church service where the offerings were taken in chits (as the settlers had no ready cash on them), polo continued.

Almost everyone who could ride male or female young or old were roped in to take part. Many of the ponies naturally disliked being hit about the legs with mallets or in the face by a bouncing wooden ball. They often stopped or shied unseating their riders so the practice games were slow and precarious but exciting.

Elspeth though only 14 years old was earning a few pennies by reporting on the hunts and polo matches, which took place with great gusto in and around Nairobi at this time, honing her skills as a future writer.

Northrup had given up big game hunting; instead he had become increasingly interested in photography. In 1921 he first met Osa and Martin Johnson, an American married couple, who were pioneer wildlife photographers and filmmakers.[222] They had rented a house just down the street from Chiromo and in between travels would return to the dark room Martin had set up there and develop their negatives and movie films. Northrup, who was always interested in anyone hailing from the United States, struck up a friendship. According to Martin he was fascinated by photography and spent many hours with him in the dark room talking with him and watching him as he worked.[223] Martin was grateful for Northrup's kindly advice and wrote that he was much indebted to him for the success of that first visit.

In 1924 the Johnsons returned to Kenya. With sponsorship from Eastman Kodak, they intended to set up a base at Lake Paradise in Marsabit, from which to photograph the habitat and lives of the animals

Osa and Martin Johnson on safari.

222 Martin Johnson (1884-1937) and Osa Johnson (1894-1953) both came from Kansas. They captured the public's imagination through their films and books of adventure in faraway exotic lands. As a result of their first Africa Expedition in 1921-1922, they made the film Trailing Wild African Animals, which was well received in the States. They raised money and sponsorship for the second trip by showing the film and giving talks and writing books about their adventures.
223 Martin Johnson, *Camera Trails in Africa*,(1924), 45.

and make wildlife films.[224] They had stumbled upon the lake by accident on their first visit, while travelling in Northern Kenya, and had been so impressed by its idyllic setting and wild beauty that they named it Lake Paradise. Upon arrival in Nairobi in February 1924, Martin made Northrup his Power of Attorney in case anything happened to them on the trip. He was always concerned about the safety and well being of his younger and charming wife Osa and would get anxious if she was late back from hunting or fishing for dinner. She was an excellent shot and enjoyed safari life. Her carefree, happy-go-lucky nature comes through in her most famous book *Four years in Paradise* published in 1941 after the tragic death of Martin in a plane crash, which she survived.

Northrup's last safari was a visit to see the Johnsons at Lake Paradise. Osa and Martin had arrived in Marsabit in April 1924 with all their equipment and had begun immediately to make themselves comfortable. They built simple houses for themselves and their staff using logs, vines and thatch found in the forest. Martin set up a laboratory, where he could develop his negatives, and built a store to keep his rolls of precious film and cameras safe. He had brought twenty cameras with him, and five of the motion picture cameras were of the type designed by Carl Akeley specifically for animal photography, and could be mounted on the back of a vehicle and taken on safari. Osa planted a vegetable garden, laboriously importing sand in gunnysacks to get the required loam mixture for the soil, and experimented with homemade bricks to make an oven. When the McMillans arrived soon after the arrival of the first mails – containing early Christmas presents – they found a perfect picture of domesticity in the jungle.

Osa describes how a runner came one morning with the news that Sir Northrup and Lady McMillan were on their way to Lake Paradise. They had taken five-and-a-half days to reach Marsabit and arrived in the evening with four big Cadillac cars with double wheels on the back axles. They were the Johnsons' first visitors.

Northrup particularly enjoyed the pancakes with Vermont syrup he

224 They stayed at Lake Paradise from 1924-1927 and made various movies and one famous film entitled Simba King of the Beasts.

had the next morning for breakfast and asked for more, despite Lucie's disapproval. Osa prepared six to eight course dinners each of the four nights they stayed. Northrup was a great eater and Osa wrote that she could almost believe his natives' boast that he ate two antelopes a day and rode on four mules at a time. She says her staff nicknamed him 'Big Stomach.' His wife tried to limit his eating but with little success, as he had an insatiable appetite. Lucie was a keen gardener and much admired Osa's garden and helped pick the vegetables for the meals. She was impressed with how big the melons, tomatoes and the strawberries had grown and took seeds for her own garden.

One evening they surprised a leopard crouching near the storehouse. Northrup said it reminded him of the good old days at Juja when lion would come right up to the doorstep. He reminisced about Africa, animals and photography, and Osa affectionately called him a grand old man, although he was only just 52. One evening they went down to the lakeside to watch the animals as one by one they came in to drink. On another evening Martin put on a movie film, as a special treat. Sir Northrup watched it with intense interest. At the end he said, "These pictures are the eighth wonder of the world. You have no idea what they will mean to the world one day as a scientific and educational record." The Johnsons were encouraged by his sincere appreciation and praise and felt their struggles and hardships were all worthwhile.

Osa had a soft spot for Northrup and was sorry to see them go. She described how their cars were enclosed in heavy wire mesh to make them lion proof and air mattresses and electric droplights were installed in two of them so that Northrup and his wife could safari in comfort after dark. In this way they could sleep under the stars, without the effort of putting up a tent and could stop wherever the fancy took. As Osa writes, they liked safari life and were always driving off "into the blue."

"We're going to come back again in a few months and we'll stay longer next time," Sir Northrup promised. But of course he never came and that was the last time they saw him.[225]

---

225 Osa Johnson, *Four Years in Paradise* (1941), 170-174.

Judy Aldrick

Northrup, who had never enjoyed good health, was now seriously unwell. He had been advised by his doctors to lose weight, but he could not. The effects of years of overeating and heavy drinking had caught up with him. His heart was now affected, his limbs swollen. He could hardly walk and was in discomfort and pain.

POSTCRIPT

AFTERMATH AND LEGACY

Northrup left Kenya for the last time on 23 February, 1925, on a passenger ship bound for Europe. On the voyage, his condition gave rise for anxiety and he was taken off the ship at Marseilles and rushed immediately to Nice where he died on Sunday 22 March, 1925, from pleurisy and heart disease. It took just six days to bring his embalmed body back to Mombasa on board the Messageries Maritime Ship the *SS Dumbea*. His coffin encased in a large crate was then taken by special coach on the train up to Nairobi accompanied by his old friend, a grief stricken Charles Bulpett.[226]

---

226 In Axel Munthe's acclaimed book *The Story of San Michele* (1929), the chapter entitled 'The Corpse Collector,' describes the death of a boy in a hotel in Heidelberg and how the body was then embalmed in great haste, placed into a soldered lead coffin, inside an outer oak coffin, and then enclosed in a packing-case for onward transportation. The body was then taken as swiftly as possible by rail and ship back to Sweden for burial. Railway regulations did not permit corpses to travel unaccompanied, so the doctor himself had to travel in a special van of the goods train with the coffin. There was a well-established system for transporting the dead.

The following morning, Monday 29 March, a long and elaborate memorial service was held at Nairobi All Saints Cathedral. Many people attended and there were hymns, eulogies and full military honours, with the last post played as the finale. The flower-covered coffin remained in the cathedral overnight and on the morning of Tuesday 30 March was taken to Donyo Sabuk, where the interment took place at three in the afternoon. As a mark of respect the flag at the Senior Commissioner's office was lowered all that day.

Lady McMillan had wired Mr E L Lindsay, the manager at Donyo Sabuk, from France with the sad news and asked him to make good the murram road up the mountain and prepare the gravesite. Lyndsay had one week to complete the preparations.[227] The chosen burial place was a flat ledge three quarters of the way up the mountainside, from which there was a panoramic view overlooking the distant plains. It was a favourite spot where Northrup had liked to sit and survey the scene and was next to the rough road that he had constructed all the way up to the summit. He had always wanted to be buried there and Northrup had built a road up Ol Donyo Sabuk, certainly before 1921, when he and Bixby had driven up to the summit.

Northrup McMillan's grave on Ol Donyo Sabuk, looking out over the African countryside at the spot where he loved to sit under the tree and admire the view.

227 Douglas Duncan, personal interview. He remembers his grandfather telling him what a rush it was to prepare the site for the burial.

One of the McMillan cars on Ol Donyo Sabuk. The radiator has boiled and has stopped for a refill on the climb up the mountain.

Recent accounts of McMillan's burial on Ol Donyo Sabuk that appear in almost all tourist guides are misleading. The story goes that he was originally meant to be buried on the top of the mountain, but that the coffin was too heavy and the tractor carrying it broke down, so the burial occurred lower down at a random spot. That is not correct. The site was chosen deliberately and organised well ahead.

The East African Standard report on the funeral makes particular mention of how arrangements were made for the difficult journey up the slopes of the mountain. Water carts were handy in case of need and teams of oxen were in readiness should a car fail on the steep ascent.

All the cars of the more than fifty mourners ascended the hill to within sixty yards of the grave. The Reverend W J Wright, accompanied by Mr J Coney, bearing the Processional Cross, and the Chief Mourners, Lady McMillan and Lieutenant Colonel and Mrs Maxwell, then advanced to the grave for the consecration of the ground. Following this the mourners approached the flower-lined grave for the funeral service. Lady McMillan placed the first wreath on the lowered coffin; other wreaths were laid covering the ground all round the grave. The Honorary pall bearers were Lord Delamere, Lord Francis Scott and

Mr CWL Bulpett, while there were 10 active pall bearers, Lt Col M Maxwell, Mr W B Thompson, Capt A T A Ritchie, Mr E L Lindsay, Capt C B Fitzgerald, Mr W G Sewell, Mr A Owen, Lt Col B Turner, Mr S Donnelly and Mr N Rushton, who lifted the large coffin and placed it into the prepared grave.

The mourners gathered round to pay their last tribute to a lost friend, companion and helper. A vast number of floral tributes surrounded the grave like a sea of vegetation. Northrup McMillan had been a highly respected member of Nairobi Society and the names listed in the newspaper read like a Who's Who of Nairobi. It was by all accounts an affectionate and impressive ceremony, high on the slopes of the mountain under the shade of a magnificent tree, with a prospect on all sides limited only by the haze of the horizon.

An early photograph shows the grave, with a temporary superstructure, next to the tree. It was Jack Everard, Lindsay's successor, who eventually ferried the huge gravestone, a single enormous slab of local granite, which remains there to this day, and placed it over the grave in 1927.[228]

View of the original magumo tree beside the grave. The tree is now gone.

Close up view of McMillan's tombstone showing where the grave was vandalised and the plaque removed.

228 Pilly Turner, personal interview. Lady McMillan later tried to plant an oak tree by the grave, but the seedling failed to grow. It was a difficult operation to transport the heavy stone up the mountain-side and place it over the grave. It was the first task Pilly's father was given when he took over as the new manager.

Nowadays Ol Donyo Sabuk is a National Park. The road, as in McMillan's day, crosses over the Athi River, which at this point is little more than a stream. Over to the right the water trickles over a picturesque series of miniature waterfalls, known as the Fourteen Falls. It is an idyllic spot, which used to be a popular picnic site. The road then heads straight for the mountain. Ol Donyo Sabuk is a Maasai name, which means fat mountain, and it sticks out of the flat plain like an enormous swelling stomach. Kilima mbogo is its Swahili name, meaning hill of the buffalo, referring to the large herd of buffalo that used to live there. The surrounding area has become a suburb of Nairobi, with new residential estates and endless development engulfing the former settler farms and open plains. Thika is now called the Birmingham of Kenya, and along the main road through what was once McMillan's land, small plots for individual houses are advertised for sale on billboards.

But the mountain remains an unspoilt beauty spot, and once through the park gates, everything remains as nature intended. Lucky Bean Trees (*erythrina abyssinica*) line the small winding road, which climbs up to the small gravesite, standing apart from and rising above the habitation and bustle of modern life. All is quiet here and the graves are not immediately recognisable, as they seem to form part of the natural landscape, the simple rough-hewn stones blending into the surroundings. Centrally placed is the enormous grave of Sir William Northrup McMillan. There is no inscription, only the flat plain stone. Surrounding it are other graves; one is Louise Decker, her inscription is still visible, but what about the others? Is one of the smaller stones covering lady Lucie and yet another Charles Bulpett perhaps?[229] All evidence has disappeared, but here once more the friends are reunited in this quiet spot overlooking the plains towards the Ngong Hills on one side and Mount Kenya on the far side of the mountain.

---

229 After Independence the graves were vandalised as it was thought that valuables would be found with the bodies, which is the reason no inscriptions remain. The ashes of Marcuswell Maxwell were buried there as well.

Judy Aldrick

An Appreciation

W.N.M.M.

Great of body, soul and heart
He does what in him lies
Fulfilling in the cause his part
He hears his country's cries

This is the first verse of a fulsome sung tribute; it goes on in increasingly sickly sentimental mode, for several more verses with excruciating rhymes finally finishing with:

So true of heart and gracious mien
Tis almost hard to find
His like in this cold world I ween
Kindness personified

Lucie McMillan appeared veiled and in full black widow's weeds, as was the custom of the time, at the memorial service and funeral, supported by her nephew Marcuswell Maxwell, with Charles Bulpett in close attendance. She was still dressed all in black when Karen Blixen reported some months later in a letter to her mother that Lucie looked terrible. (Whether this was from grief or because black did not suit her is not explained).

Northrup's will left his entire estate to his widow Lucie, provided she outlived him for more than a year. But money was tighter than it had been when her husband was alive, for although she inherited the Kenyan properties, the income from trust money in the US ceased. Under the terms of Eliza McMillan's will, the money went to the hospital in St Louis on the death of her son, when he died without issue. At one point Lucie had to borrow money from Bixby and she was involved in a court case about her investments, which had been mishandled. A number of economies were made at Ol

Donyo Sabuk and Chiromo to put them on a more business like footing. Lucie's nephew Lt Col Maxwell was the chief trustee of the Kenyan will. He was her closest relative and heir and helped her with the running of the estates. She also relied heavily on the financial expertise and advice of W C Hunter her accountant, who she had known for several years and was a good friend.[230]

Lucie was still an extremely wealthy woman and all was not doom and gloom. She did not marry again, but continued to enjoy her safaris, international travel, and to entertain friends and go to the races. She also decided to direct her energies towards building a fitting memorial to her husband in Kenya. This was to be a splendid library in Nairobi, as it had always been her husband's wish during his lifetime to provide a place "where tired minds could find refreshment" and what could be more appropriate than a library, which would nourish the mental development of the colony.

The new library benefited from the Carnegie Trust, which had undertaken to supply most of the books and the intention was that the Nairobi library would be the first of a system of rural libraries to be built throughout the colony. Lucie McMillan generously agreed to provide the reference books for the Nairobi library.

The foundation stone was laid in 1929 and the project was blessed by a canon from the cathedral.

The small ceremony was headed by the Acting Governor Sir Jacob Barth and attended by a small but distinguished gathering.[231] Lord Delamere was there and Mr Legat and the Mayor of Nairobi made speeches praising Northrup McMillan and his contribution

---

230 William Clark Hunter came to Kenya in 1906 and established the firm of WC Hunter Accountants. This grew to be a leading commercial enterprise in the colony and was later purchased by Dalgety & Co. Hunter was an unofficial member for Leg Co and sat on the Sisal Board for many years. He was married to Dorothy Grogan, Major Grogan's sister.

231 Sir Jacob William Barth came to Kenya in 1902 as the Registrar of the High Court based in Mombasa. He later moved to Nairobi, became a judge, and sat on the Land Commission and the Labour Commission. He was a good friend of the McMillans.

to the colony. Mr A A Legat[232] said that Northrup's heart was as big as his great frame and described how, "No institution of use to mankind went without his support and no individual appealed to him for help in vain." He declared: "He went about doing good by

Laying the foundation stone of the Mc-Millan Memorial Library in 1929. Lady McMillan is sitting in the centre with Charles Bulpett beside her.

stealth! And on one's journey through life one seldom meets with such devotion to the service of one's fellow man." The mayor thanked Lady McMillan for the valuable addition to the amenities of the capital and mentioned how important education was for stimulating progress. Two years later in 1931 the library was formally opened by Sir Joseph Byrne.

The McMillan Memorial Library still exists today in central Nairobi. It is a familiar landmark of the town. It was designed by

The official opening of the McMillan Memorial Library in 1931.

232 Arthur A Legat came to Kenya in 1912 as the Manager of the Bank of India and was a Nairobi banker, who knew Northrup well. He was also a member of the Chamber of Commerce.

The McMillan Memorial Library in 2011 in busy downtown Nairobi.

The stone lions that flank the library steps were donated by Sir John and Lady Harrington in memory of their cousin Northrup.

Rand Overy and built by George Blowers in classical style. Stone steps flanked by lions, given by Sir John and Lady Harrington in memory of Northrup, lead up to the grand portico entrance.

In the large reading room on the ground floor, there are statuettes in the corners and elegant light fittings over the large wooden tables to provide a cultural ambience to inspire the readers. A bust of Sir Northrup graces one wall and some of the furnishings came from Karen Blixen's house contents sale, which Lucie bought up for the library. Originally open to Europeans only, it is now patronised by all races and still provides a quiet place to read in downtown Nairobi. In the basement are newspapers and on the top floor is the Africana section, where you can still find books originating from the McMillan's personal library.[233]

233 "The McMillan Memorial Library Built in Nairobi," Old Africa Issue 38, December 2011-January 2012, 5-6.

The Duke of Aosta (second from the left) and Lady McMillan (second from the right) on Old Donyo Sabuk. After the defeat of the Italian army in Abyssinia, The Duke of Aosta was interned at Ol Donyo Sabuk House in 1941. Peter Maxwell, the eventual heir to the McMillan Kenyan properties, is standing on the right.

Northrup McMillan's legacy to Kenya was extensive although largely forgotten today. The McMillan Library, which bears his name, is the most well-known and visible, but Chiromo estate left to the University of Nairobi and Ol Donyo Sabuk left to the nation as a national park were also charitable gifts of immeasurable value, which have stood the test of time. Less well known are Laikipia Road, which used to be called McMillan road, as he provided the funds to build it, and the Scott Sanatorium at Kijabe, which closed in the 1920s, but in its day gave important assistance to sick settlers and wounded soldiers. Other institutions, which owed much to Northrup's initial input include the Nairobi YMCA, the EAWL, and the first African teacher training college at Kabete. They are all still functioning well, although Northrup's connection with them is now lost in the mists of time. Quietly and by stealth he helped wherever he could, unassuming and generous, like his parents, ever serving others as his school training had taught him. Great wealth also brought great responsibilities and he understood that. What he took from Kenya, he tried to pay back. He used his large fortune to invest in farming ventures, businesses and training projects. Kenya benefited and was the richer for hosting Northrup.

Besides his tangible legacies, Northrup was also instrumental in introducing the fashion for wildlife safaris, with safari lodges and game parks. He helped to popularise Kenya as a tourist destination particularly amongst Americans. His Juja ranch was a hunter's paradise and a byword for luxury and hospitality, known to the international hunting fraternity and a blueprint for later safari tourism. Often his ideas were ahead of the times. He seemed impractical and over optimistic, but his failures prepared the way for others to learn by his mistakes. His Blue Nile exploration and gold mining are two such examples of this trend, while his farms, though unprofitable during his lifetime, provided many with work and a stepping-stone to businesses of their own.

His good will and benign presence, more than his rhetoric, served him well in politics. His constituents believed in his sincerity of purpose and appreciated his generosity and voted for him. He sat on the war council and on occasion, the executive council, the highest body in the land and had his hand on the steering wheel of the country at a time of momentous change and development.

Lord Delamere and Ewart Grogan are always seen as the two big men of pioneer settler politics in Kenya, but Northrup McMillan, had he lived a few more years may well have joined them on the podium. He was the silent partner of the triumvirate, the third man, whose generosity and ever flowing funds enabled policies to be acted upon. He provided support and encouragement when it was needed. He was the colleague and true friend who was prepared to remain in the background, who understood the value of self sacrifice when a larger goal was in sight and could stand aside to let those with greater abilities forge ahead for the greater

*Lady Lucie McMillan is presented
to Princess Elizabeth in Nairobi in 1952.*

good. He was self-effacing and a man of few words, but yet he enjoyed being in the public eye and liked being involved in great affairs and basking in the adulation of his peers.

Seemingly unpromising as a youth, his character was one that improved with age. His attributes of kindliness and generosity, of friendship and cheerfulness, did not appeal to his businesslike father, who wanted business acumen and scholastic achievement from his only son, but were recognised for their worth later in life. His personal wealth was used to do good and to help others and Kenya was the chief beneficiary.

In the end it was the huge size and wealth of Northrup McMillan that provided the most enduring image of the man and for which he is chiefly remembered in Kenya. His impressive personal appearance engraved itself indelibly upon the minds of all those who met him. As the stories were told, they were embroidered and at each succeeding telling, he became fatter and larger and richer. The myth of the enormous Lord McMillan, seven feet tall and so fat and heavy that the tractor could not drag his body up the mountain, has been perpetuated and with it the image of a man, who was so rich he owned a mountain as well as huge estates. His early travels in Ethiopia and Sudan have all but been forgotten and his generous deeds discounted. Most written accounts have focussed on Juja and have portrayed him as a hedonistic, pleasure seeker, a wealthy playboy, who used the country as a playground for his own gratification and omit his more worthy endeavours. The well publicised scandals of The Happy Valley Set have tended to tar all Kenya settlers with the same brush, and it is easy to believe the worst and think that most behaved in the same manner, which they did not.

Northrup McMillan, who left no heirs to set the record straight and who was born American but became British, has had few defenders to insist the truth be told and his reputation has suffered as a result. Neither fully American nor completely British, he was not from an aristocratic background, but gained a title while living in Kenya. As such Northrup does not fall into the accepted Kenya colonial settler pattern – he is a hybrid species – the exception which proves the rule. Considered up until now a minor player in the history of Kenyan colonial settlement, worthy of little more than a paragraph or a passing mention in the history books, he has been largely ignored. As he left no personal papers or defining footprint, his story has been difficult to unravel but no less rewarding or fascinating for that. While writing this biography I have felt at times rather like a hunter stalking an elusive prey, which sometimes disappears into the undergrowth only to then appear on a distant plain, or pop up somewhere entirely unexpected. I hope that this account will have brought to life the man as he was and the era in which he lived and that I have succeeded in dispelling the shadows and misconceptions that have lingered round him.

Kenya is one of the few sub-Saharan African countries, which has maintained a stable and moderate democratic government, with good international relations. This is in part due the special circumstances of its colonial background, particularly the early period, when officials, pioneering settlers and local leaders worked together to lay the solid foundations from which a modern Kenya could grow and thrive. These cooperative early beginnings were important for the ultimate success of the country and Kenya was also fortunate in its first colonial administrators and colonists. The pioneering settlers who were initially attracted to the country proved to be men of ability, with vision and investment funds, and Northrup belonged to this early group. Much of his enormous fortune was spent in Kenya and whether at Juja, or on his experimental farms, or at the very heart of government debate, he contributed to the development of present day Kenya and Sir William Northrup McMillan deserves to be remembered.

Northrup

Index

Nuer 79, 81, 84

O

Ol Donyo Sabuk 15, 19, 22, 23, 74,
    98, 100, 102, 113, 196, 197,
    200, 203, 204, 209, 210, 224,
    225, 227, 228, 232, 242
Olea 84
Oromo 75
Overy, Rand 231
Owen, A 197, 226

P

Parklands 127, 138, 146
Peek, Sir Wilfred 156
Penton 196
Pibor 82
Pixley, Jack 138
Pokum 84, 89
Pugh, Canon & Mrs 194, 198, 199

Q

Quatermain, Allan 25, 42, 53

R

Rainey, Paul 131
Regel 197
Ringer, Major 98, 99, 101, 117, 129,
    143, 158
Ritchie, Capt A T A 226
Roosevelt, Kermit 121, 123, 127, 128
Roosevelt, Theodore (Teddy) 7, 16,
    43, 60, 120, 121, 122, 123, 124,
    125, 126, 127, 128, 129, 133,
    134, 135, 154, 157, 158, 159,
    166, 168, 171
Royal Geographical Society 8, 61, 73,
    90, 107, 167
Ruiru 116, 164
Rushton, N 226

S

Sadler, Sir James Hayes 138, 147
Salim, Sir Ali bin 192
Samburu 96, 133
Scott, L C 100
Scott Sanatorium 142, 232
Scott, Sir Henry Harold 142
Sehof, Clara 76
Selous, Frederick Courteney 13, 17,
    41, 42, 43, 53, 107, 122, 123,
    132, 133, 134, 154, 157, 165,
    166, 171, 172, 173, 202
Sewell, W F 226
Shilluk 79, 80
Singer, Dr Charles 75
Singh, Mr 200, 201
Skinner, Robert 60
Smith Academy, St Louis 31
Smuts, General 18, 171, 185
Sobat 14, 56, 72, 74, 77, 80, 82, 122
Stanley, Henry Morton 43, 44, 88, 176
Stewart, Brigadier General James M
    165
Stewart, Sir Donald 97, 106, 146
St Louis 6, 8, 13, 14, 16, 17, 18, 21,
    27, 28, 29, 30, 31, 32, 36, 38,
    40, 45, 46, 47, 48, 49, 50, 51,
    60, 61, 86, 121, 150, 151, 156,
    157, 158, 159, 162, 163, 164,
    165, 191, 192, 194, 228
St Louis Union Trust Company 191
Strange, Nora 213
Stranracr 27
Swedo-Coffee Company 145
Swift, Randall 78

T

Tacalin, Shaka 85
Taitu, Empress 86
Tanga 163, 172, 174

242

Tarlton, Leslie 112, 177
Taru 95, 96
Tasamma, Ras 86
Taveta 161, 163, 171, 174
The Hill School 8, 32, 33
Thompson, W B 226
Thornburgh, Edwine 156, 157
Thuku, Harry 186, 205, 206
Toogood, J J 168
Towell 74, 101
Turi 167
Turner, Lt Col B 8, 19, 192, 202, 203,
    206, 210, 226
Turner, Pilly 8, 19, 192, 202, 203, 206,
    210, 226

U

Ukamba 178, 189, 190, 192

V

Voi 96, 163, 166

W

Ward, Freddy 161
Watt, Gertrude 107
Watts, Stewart 195
Wavell, Major 161
Webber, George 47
Webber, Lucie 46, 47
White, Edward Stewart 114, 117, 143,
    168, 197
Wilhelm, Prince of Sweden 16, 131,
    145
Wingate, Col Reginald 57, 101
Wood, Tommy 148, 184
Wood-Winterton Agreement 187
Wright, The Rev W J 225

Y

Yambo 84

Young Kikuyu Association 186
Young, W D 99

Z

Zaphiro, Philip Photius Constantine
    75, 85, 88, 89

Judy Aldrick